SPEAKING
BORICUA!

by Jared Romey

SPEAKING
BORICUA!

by Jared Romey

Publicaciones
Puertorriqueñas
EDITORES

Créditos editoriales
Segunda edición, 2006
Primera edición, 2005

Prohibida la reproducción total o parcial de esta obra por cualquier medio técnico,
mecánico o electrónico sin previo permiso escrito por parte de Publicaciones
Puertorriqueñas, Inc.

© Publicaciones Puertorriqueñas, Inc.
© Jared Romey

ISBN 0-934369-16-X

Producido en Puerto Rico
Impreso por Panamericana
Formas e Impresos S.A.
Quién sólo actúa como impresor
Impreso en Colombia   Printed in Colombia

Editor:
ANDRÉS PALOMARES
Diseño Tipográfico: gotay@publicacionespr.com
EVA GOTAY PASTRANA
Diseño Tipográfico:
HILDA NUEZ
Portada:
HENRY D'AZA
Departamento Multimedia: negron@publicacionespr.com
CARLOS NEGRÓN
Director de impresos en Puerto Rico
XAVIER MOLINA
Negativos y separación de colores
PUBLICACIONES PUERTORRIQUEÑAS
Facturación
BERENICE DE LA CRUZ
Almacén y Distribución
LUIS J. BENÍTEZ • REINALDO DÍAZ
Departamento de Ventas: dventas@publicacionespr.com
ANA CAMACHO   STEPHANI NAVARRO
NÉLIDA IRIZARRY   NEIDA APONTE

Publicaciones Puertorriqueñas, Inc.
Calle Mayagüez 44
Hato Rey, Puerto Rico 00919
Tel. (787) 759-9673 Fax (787) 250-6498
e-mail: pubpr@coqui.net

Para Mike y Polli...

amigos, maestros y, sobre todo, padres pacientes

For Mike and Polli...

friends, teachers and, above all, patient parents

When people travel here from across the country, they shed jealousies and politics and prejudices... The mighty climb down. The humble are elevated.

Hugh Sidey

ÍNDICE / *INDEX*

Introducción/ Introduction

Cuando me mudé a Puerto Rico, ya hablaba español fluido, pues había viajado y vivido en Latinoamérica extensamente, y estaba bastante seguro de que mi traslado a Puerto Rico sería fácil. ¡Qué tonto fui! Me tomó más de un mes para entender qué es un **mahón**, y mucho, mucho más para entender **mé-ká-wé-ná** (yo sé, que este ejemplo es complicado...trata de pronunciarlo en voz alta). Han pasado más de dos años y aún diariamente encuentro nuevas palabras.

La idea surgió un día cuando yo pensé que sería divertido crear una lista de palabras (no te preocupes, no eres la única persona que ha pensado que mi sentido de diversión es raro) que eran nuevas para mí. Comencé escuchando a la gente hablar durante el almuerzo, leyendo el periódico, o solamente siguiendo las conversaciones de amigos en las salidas de noche, para agregar a La Lista. La mayoría del tiempo nuevas palabras (para mí) salieron en las conversaciones. Sin embargo, mis "víctimas" no tenían idea de que yo los estaba estudiando. Esto me permitió observar el idioma en su uso diario, crudo y sin editar.

De vez en cuando, haré referencia al "idioma puertorriqueño." Esta es una frase no-técnica que utilizo

para referirme al uso particular del idioma español en
Puerto Rico. Elegí el título Speaking Boricua! porque esta
particularidad casi amerita su propio nombre. Por ende, lo
considero el idioma moderno Boricua!

Algunas frases y palabras no son únicas de Puerto
Rico. He creado esta lista, en gran parte, basándome en
mis experiencias con el español, específicamente en
México, Chile, Argentina y Puerto Rico.

Al mismo tiempo, no tengo la intención de crear un
tomo exhaustivo del idioma o de los modismos
puertorriqueños. Solamente quiero presentar una guía para
ayudar a los visitantes de Puerto Rico, a los puertorriqueños
que se criaron fuera de Puerto Rico, y a los puertorriqueños
nativos.

He incluido secciones cortas de gramática y
pronunciación para la persona (como yo) que realmente
disfruta de estas cosas. En mi opinion, se pueden apreciar
mejor las sutilezas de cualquier idioma después de entender
la gramática y la pronunciación local.

Los idiomas son criaturas vivas y que respiran, cada
uno con su propio carácter y personalidad; también proveen
una forma estupenda para entender una cultura y su gente.
Pero, más importante aún, entretienen.

Espero que esto te haga sonreír.

When I first moved to Puerto Rico, I already spoke Spanish fluently, had traveled and lived in Latin America extensively, and was quite sure that my move to Puerto Rico would be an easy transition. What a fool I was! It took me over month to figure out what a **mahón** is, and much, much longer to understand **mé-ká-wé-ná** (I know, this one's tricky...try saying it out loud). It's now more than two years later, and I'm still picking up new words every day.

The idea started one day when I thought it would be fun to keep a list of words (don't worry, you aren't the only person that thinks I have a warped sense of fun) that were new to me. I began listening to lunch conversations, reading the newspaper, or just following the conversations of friends at late-night gatherings, to add to The List. More often than not new words (to me) popped up in conversations. Just as often, my "victims" had no idea that they were being studied. This allowed me to observe the language in its raw, unedited daily usage.

I may occasionally refer to "the Puerto Rican language." This is a non-technical phrase I use in reference to the uniqueness that has developed within the Spanish language in Puerto Rico. I chose the title Speaking Boricua! because this uniqueness almost merits its own name. Thus, the naming of the modern language, Boricuan!

Some of these words and phrases are not specific only to Puerto Rico. I have compiled this list largely based on my personal experiences with Spanish, specifically in Mexico, Chile, Argentina and Puerto Rico.

At the same time, this is not meant to be a definitive source on Puerto Rican language or slang. I just want to put together a guide to help visitors to Puerto Rico, Puerto Ricans who grew up outside of Puerto Rico, and even native Puerto Ricans.

I have included short sections on grammar and pronunciation for the occasional person (like myself) that actually enjoys these things. In my opinion, the nuances in any language can be better appreciated once the local grammar and pronunciation are understood.

Languages are creatures that live and breathe, each with its own character and personality; they also provide a wonderful understanding of a culture and its people. But most importantly, they entertain.

I hope this makes you smile.

Reconocimientos/ Acknowledgements

E l proceso que me llevó a desarrollar este libro realmente empezó en 1997 cuando me mudé a Chile, mucho antes de que conociera Puerto Rico. Mis queridas amigas chilenas, con mucha paciencia, dedicaron tiempo a enseñarme su idioma y las idiosincracias que lleva el español chileno. Con ellas, aprendí a disfrutar el idioma. Esto despertó mi interés en entender el idioma en cada país que posteriormente he conocido. Por toda su paciencia durante mis años allá, quiero agradecer a Andrea, Claudia B., Claudia N., Jessica, La Guera, Pamela, Rosa Estér, Teresita y Verónica.

No puedo pensar en Chile sin pensar en Evelyn. Gracias... de mi corazón.

Aquí en Puerto Rico, como mencioné previamente, hay varias personas que nunca se dieron cuenta de que hacían contribuciones al libro. Me encantó escucharlos y tomar notas. Sus contribuciones no tienen precio. Aprendí muchísimo de ellos.

Aparte de las investigaciones incógnitas que hice, Arkel, Bertha, Diana, Laura e Ivelisse me ayudaron a entender el vocabulario boricua. Y para el punto de vista extranjero, no puedo olvidarme de Gabriela y Ute.

También, necesito mencionar mi abuela, Dorothy Main, quien a través de los juegos de Scrabble, me introdujo al placer que produce el conocer bien y usar correctamente un idioma.

Finalmente, quiero agradecer a Brenda Latorre, la persona clave, desde el principio, en la creación de este libro. Sin la ayuda y (de nuevo) la paciencia de ella, yo no hubiera logrado completar este libro. Al mismo tiempo la familia de ella me ofreció una vista isleña del idioma.

¡Gracias a todos!

The first steps that started this book really began in 1997 when I moved to Chile, even before knowing anything about Puerto Rico. My dear Chilean friends took the time, mixed with lots of patience, to teach me the idiosyncracies of Chilean Spanish. With them I learned to enjoy the language. That heated up in me an interest to understand the language from each country in which I have subsequently lived. For all their patience during my years there, I want to thank Andrea, Claudia B., Claudia N., Jessica, La Guera, Pamela, Rosa Estér, Teresita y Verónica.

I cannot think of Chile without thinking of Evelyn. Thank you...from the bottom of my heart.

Here in Puerto Rico, as I previously mentioned, there are various people that never realized they were contributing to this book. I loved listening to them and taking notes. Their contributions are priceless. I learned a lot from them.

Apart from the clandestine investigations, Arkel, Bertha, Diana, Laura and Ivelisse helped me understand the Boricua vocabulary. And for the foreign point of view I can't leave out Gabriela and Ute.

I also need to mention my grandmother, Dorothy Main, who, with the games of Scrabble, introduced me to the pleasure that comes from learning a language well and using it correctly.

Finally, the most important thanks belongs to Brenda Latorre, the key person, from the beginning, in the creation of this book. Without her help and (again) patience, I would never have finished it. At the same time, her family also contributed, with an island perspective of Boricuan.

Thank you to everyone!

How To Use This Lexicon

First of all, this book should be used as a basis for enjoying a visit to, living in, or even just, learning about Puerto Rico. In no way should this lexicon be seen as an academic, literary or reference work on the language.

The words (I will use *word* in a general sense whose meaning also includes phrases so as not to always repeat *word/phrase*) in this book will be written, whenever possible, similar to their pronunciation (ex. *abombao* and *malcriao*, although the correct spellings are *abombado* and *malcriado*). Every once in a while, however, it is not possible to list a word as it is pronounced, because the pronunciation is so far off from the actual word (*ex. me ká wé ná*, correctly written as *me cago en nada*).

Throughout the lexicon the following abbreviations have been used to facilitate the understanding and uses of words:

Abbreviation	Meaning
alt. sp.	Alternate Spelling
ex.	Example
exp.	Expression

o/a	Masculine or Feminine
pl.	Plural
pr.	Pronunciation
sl.	Slang
syn.	Synonym

Besides the above abbreviations, the following symbols are located before a word's entry and are to help make the lexicon a bit easier to enjoy (NOTE: The symbol may apply to only one definition for words with more than one definition). The four symbols are:

★   Commonly used words

🍽   Food related words

💣   Words that may not be acceptable in some circumstances, including expletives, insulting, crude or politically incorrect words.

☺   English root words or words that have a relationship to English.

Example 1:

★💣 **anda pál cará (anda para el carajo):** 1. damn, darn; used when you forget something or did something. 2. exp. to communicate surprise or disbelief.

In Example 1 the two symbols (★ ✹) clarify the usage of the phrase. Following the symbols in **bold** is the phrase which has been written as pronounced. Then in parentheses is the correct written form of the phrase. In the case of a word that has more than one definition, each definition is marked by its corresponding number, and then followed by the definition.

Example 2:

le dieron hasta por dentro del pelo: literally "they gave it to him even inside his hair", see *le dieron como a pillo de película.*

In the text of Example 2, the information within the quotation marks is a direct translation from Spanish. This is included when the exact translation help clarifies the meaning of the text, or offers a touch of humor. Also in this example, in *italics*, is a reference to another phrase, which provides a synonym of the phrase as well as give a more detailed definition.

Example 3:

★ ✹ **cafre:** (syn. *charro*) refers to a person that speaks using many expletives, a person that dresses cheaply (like a prostitute), or a person that speaks in an uneducated form; it is an insult for someone to be called *cafre.*

For Example 3, the parentheses (syn. *charro*) following the word entry in **bold** reference another entry in the lexicon that is a synonym for this word. In the main text of the definition, parentheses are used to give more detail for a definition or an example to help clarify the definition.

Cómo Usar Este Léxico

Primero que nada, este libro sirve para aprovechar una visita a, para acostumbrarse a vivir en, o solamente para aprender sobre Puerto Rico. De ninguna forma, está escrito este léxico para servir como un texto académico, literario o de referencia sobre el idioma puertorriqueño.

Las palabras (usaré *palabra* en forma general para incluir no solamente las palabras, sino también las frases en este libro. De este modo no tendré que repetir palabra/frase cada vez) en este libro están escritas, cuando es posible, según su pronunciación (ej. *abombao* y *malcriao*, aunque las formas correctas son *abombado* y *malcriado*). De vez en cuando, no será posible incluir una palabra como se pronuncia, porque la pronunciación es muy diferente a la palabra escrita (ej. *me ká wé ná*, correctamente escrita como *me cago en nada*).

En este lexico, se usan las siguientes abreviaturas para facilitar entender y usar las palabras:

Abreviatura	Significado
alt. sp.	Ortografía alternativa
ex.	Ejemplo
exp.	Dicho o Expresión

o/a	Masculino o Femenino
pl.	Plural
pr.	Pronunciación
sl.	Modismo
syn.	Sinónimo

Aparte de las abreviaturas, los siguientes símbolos están localizados antes de la palabra o frase y facilitan el uso del léxico (NOTA: El símbolo puede aplicarse solamente a una definición, en caso de que que la palabra tenga más de una definición). Los cuatros símbolos son:

★ Palabras comunes

🍽 Palabras relacionadas con comida

💣 Palabras que, quizás, no serán aceptables en algunas circunstancias. Incluye malas palabras, palabras insultantes o palabras que pueden ofender a algunas personas o grupos de personas.

☺ Palabras que tienen una base o alguna relación con el inglés

Ejemplo 1:

★ 💣 **anda pál cará (anda para el carajo)***:* 1. damn, darn; used when you forget something or did something. 2. exp. to communicate surprise or disbelief.

En el Ejemplo 1 los dos símbolos (★ 💣) clarifican el uso de la frase. Siguiendo los símbolos en **negrita**, está la frase como se pronuncia. Luego de eso, en paréntesis, se encuentra la frase correctamente escrita. En el caso de una palabra con más de una definición, cada definición aparece con un número correspondiente, seguido por la definición.

Ejemplo 2:

le dieron hasta por dentro del pelo: literally "they gave it to him even inside his hair", see *le dieron como a pillo de película.*

En el texto del Ejemplo 2, la información dentro de las comillas es una traducción directa del español. Se incluye esto cuando la traducción exacta aclara el sentido del texto, o cuando ofrece un poco de humor a la frase. También en este ejemplo, en *cursiva*, hay una referencia a otra frase que sirve de sinónimo y al mismo tiempo ofrece una definición más detallada de la frase.

Ejemplo 3:

★ ❦cafre: (*syn. charro*) refers to a person that speaks using many expletives, a person that dresses cheaply (like a prostitute), or a person that speaks in an uneducated form; it is an insult for someone to be called *cafre*.

En el Ejemplo 3, los parentesis (*syn. charro*) que siguen la palabra en **negrita** se refieren a un sinónimo de la palabra, con su propia definición en el léxico. En el texto principal de la definición, los paréntesis proveen más detalles acerca de la definición, o un ejemplo para aclarar la definición.

Grammar & Usage

As in most countries, several unique grammar adaptations have appeared over the years in Puerto Rico. While sometimes these usages are grammatically incorrect, they are so widespread that they are accepted as being correct. Below are examples:

1. The most common "mistake" in Puerto Rican Spanish is to mix English with Spanish in the same sentence, sometimes known as Spanglish.

    Ex. Estaba lloviendo <u>so</u> yo compré una sombrilla.

2. For the 2nd person singular, past tense (preterite) the correct conjugation of a verb is *-aste* or *-iste* (*ex. hablaste, comiste*). You will hear people sometimes add an extra letter S to the end of the conjugated verb.

    Ex. me llamastes (me llamaste), me dijistes (me dijiste)

3. Again, in the 2nd person singular, past tense (preterite) the verb *traer* is almost always incorrectly conjugated as *traiste*. The correct conjugation is *trajiste*. The same mistake exists for the 1st person pl.; *trajimos* is the correct

conjugation instead of the incorrectly used *traimos*.

4. Several phrases have been directly translated from English into Spanish.

   Ex. Te llamo para atrás. (I'll call you back), Te veo (See you).

5. The subject is often placed in incorrectly in front of the verb as in phrases like *¿Quién tú eres?* and *¿Cómo tú estás?* The correct form is *¿Quién eres tú?* or *¿Cómo estás tú?*

6. The phrase *no me di de cuenta* is used incorrectly, instead of the correct phrase *no me di cuenta de*. The preposition *de* must be after the substantive *cuenta*.

7. The phrase *más ninguno* is often incorrectly used to signify nothing else or nothing more. The correct Spanish phrase is *ningún otro*. Similarly, *más nada* is correctly expressed as *nada más*.

8. The verb *haber* in the past tense is sometimes mistakenly conjugated in the pl. form as *habían* instead of the correct form *había*.

   *Ex. **Habían** tres personas esperando la guagua esta mañana. (**Había** tres personas esperando la guagua esta mañana.)*

9. The phrase *el más que sabe* is used incorrectly, instead of the correct phrase *el que más sabe*.

10. * The diminutive suffix **ITO** is sometimes added to words to express small size. It is also used as an expression of esteem or caring for someone.

    Ex. Amiguito, ven a verme esta tarde para tomar un café.

11. The phrase *más que uno* is often incorrectly used to mean only one instead of the correct form *solamente uno*.

    Ex. Ayer fui a comprar dos maletas nuevas, pero solamente queda más que uno, así que no compré nada. (Ayer fui a comprar dos maletas nuevas, pero solamente queda una, así que no compré nada.)

*Note: While this is gramatically correct, it has been included to clarify its usages.

Gramática

Como en la mayoría de los países, varias adaptaciones gramaticales únicas para Puerto Rico se han desarrollado con el paso del tiempo. Aunque a veces estas adaptaciones son gramaticalmente incorrectas, son tan comunes que logran ser aceptadas en el idioma.

Abajo encontrarán algunos ejemplos:

1. El "error" más común en el español de Puerto Rico es mezclar el inglés con el español en la misma frase. Esto se conoce a veces como Spanglish.

   Ej. Estaba lloviendo __so__ yo compré una sombrilla.

2. La conjugación de un verbo en segunda persona singular, pretérito es *-aste* o *-iste*. (*ej. hablaste, comiste*). En Puerto Rico se agrega a veces la letra *S* al final del verbo conjugado.

   Ej. me llamastes (me llamaste), me dijistes (me dijiste)

3. El verbo *traer* en segunda persona singular, pretérito es casi siempre incorrectamente conjugado como *traiste*. La conjugación correcta es *trajiste*. Se comete el mismo error al conjugar

la primera persona pl.: *trajimos* es la conjugación correcta mientras que *traimos* es la forma erróneamente usada.

4. Varias frases han sido directamente traducidas del inglés al español.

   Ej. Te llamo para atrás (I'll call you back), Te veo (See you).

5. Muchas veces se pone incorrectamente el sujeto antes del verbo como en *¿Quién tú eres?* y *¿Cómo tú estas?* La forma adecuada de decirlo es: *¿Quién eres tú?* o *¿Cómo estas tú?*

6. La frase *no me di de cuenta* es incorrectamente usada para significar *no me di cuenta de*. La preposición *de* no se debe anteponer al sustantivo *cuenta*.

7. La frase *más ninguno* es incorrectamente usada para significar *ningún otro*. Parecido a este caso es la frase *más nada*, que correctamente debe decir *nada más*.

8. La conjugación del verbo *haber* en imperfecto se usa erróneamente en pl. como *habían* en vez de la forma correcta *había*.

   *Ej. **Habían** tres personas esperando la guagua esta mañana. (**Había** tres personas esperando la guagua esta mañana).*

9. Se usa la frase *el más que sabe* incorrectamente en vez de la frase correcta *el que más sabe*.

10. * El sufijo diminutivo **ITO** a veces se utiliza para referirle al tamaño pequeño de una persona o de una cosa. También se utiliza para expresar afecto, aunque puede tener una connotación negativa en algunos contextos.

    Ej. Amiguito, ven a verme esta tarde para tomar un café.

11. Se usa la frase *más que uno* incorrectamente, en vez de la frase correcta *solamente uno*.

    *Ej. Ayer fui a comprar dos maletas nuevas, pero solamente queda **más que una**, así que no compré nada. (Ayer fui a comprar dos maletas nuevas, pero **solamente queda una**, así que no compré nada.)*

* Nota: Aunque es gramaticalmente correcto se incluyó debido al uso continuo del mismo.

Pronunciation

Puerto Rico, as in any other country in the world, has its own unique pronunciation for certain words, phrases and sounds. If you have only ever heard Spanish in a formal class setting or even if you are accustomed to an accent from a different country, it may take some time to understand the Puerto Rican accent when you first arrive on the island. Here are some guidelines to help that transition (words and phrases in parentheses are the correct spellings/pronunciations):

1. Words that end in the letters **ADO** will be pronounced without the letter **D**.

   Ex. amogollao (amogollado), afrentao (afrentado), eñemao (eñemado).

2. Words that end in a consonant and a vowel (ex. *pa<u>ra</u>, cara<u>jo</u>*, etc.) will be pronounced without the consonant.

   Ex. anda pá al cará (anda para el carajo), mira pá yá (mira para allá), me cá 'e ná (me cago en nada o me caso en nada).

3. Words with the letter *R* followed by a consonant
    will be pronounced as if the letter *R* were the
    letter *L*.

    Ex. Louldes (Lourdes), almas (armas).

4. Words with the letter *S* followed by a consonant
    will be pronounced as if the letter *S* were the
    letter *H*.

    Ex. ehnú (esnú), ehtartear (estartear).

5. Outside of San Juan, many people pronounce the
    double letter *RR* sound as if it were a *J* in Spanish
    and an *H* in English.

    Ex. cajo (carro).

6. For transition words such as *De* or *En*, the
    consonant is sometimes dropped.

    *Ex. me cá 'e ná (me cago en nada), pote 'e leche
    (pote de leche).*

7. The letter *P* when followed by a consonant may
    be replaced with the letter *C*.

    Ex. concecto (concepto), Pecsi (Pepsi)

8. The letter *S* is often dropped and replaced with
    an English letter *H* sound.

    *Ex. loh muertoh (los muertos), pehcadoreh
    (pescadores)*

9. The letter **R** at the end of a word is often pronounced as an English **R**. The sound comes out as a "hard"sounding letter with more emphasis than normal placed on the **R**.

   Ex. PicaR (picar).

Pronunciación

En Puerto Rico, tal como en todos los países hispanos, existe un acento particular en la pronunciación del idioma. Estas "reglas", por lo general, facilitan la rapidez con que se puede hablar el idioma. A los hablantes nativos del español esta sección les ayudará a integrarse y a entender más rápido a los puertorriqueños (las palabras y frases en parentesis son las pronunciaciones correctas):

1. Palabras que terminan en las letras **ADO** se pronuncian sin la letra **D**.

    Ej. amogollao (amogollado), afrentao (afrentado), eñemao (eñemado)

2. Palabras que terminan en una consonante y una vocal (ej. *para, carajo*, etc.) se pronuncian sin la consonante.

    Ej. anda pá al cará (anda para el carajo), mira pá yá (mira para allá), me cá 'e ná (me cago en nada).

3. Palabras con la letra **R** seguida por otra consonante se pronuncian como si la letra **R** fuera la letra **L**.

    Ej. Louldes (Lourdes), almas (armas).

4. Palabras con la letra **S** seguidas por una consonante se pronuncian como si la letra **S** fuera la letra **J**.

   Ej. ejnú (esnú), ejtartear (estartear)

5. Fuera de la region metropolitana de San Juan, mucha gente pronuncia la letra **RR** como si fuera una **J** en español o una **H** en inglés.

   Ej. cajo (carro)

6. Para palabras de transición como **De** o **En**, se elimina la consonante.

   Ej. me cá 'e ná (me cago en nada o me caso en nada), pote 'e leche (pote de leche)

7. Cuando otra consonante sigue la letra **P,** se reemplaza la **P** con una **C**.

   Ej. concecto (concepto), Pecsi (Pepsi)

8. Se reemplaza la letra **S** con la letra **J**.

   Ej. loj muertoj (los muertos), pejcadorej (pescadores)

9. Se pronuncia la letra **R** al final de una palabra como una **R** en inglés. El sonido de la letra **R** requiere un énfasis extra.

   Ej. PicaR (picar)

Lexicon: English Words

There are many words that Puerto Ricans have borrowed from English. Several times I have had more success using the English word instead of the Spanish equivalent (*Ex. tarjeta de embarque = boarding pass*). The following is a list of words that have the same meaning as in English.

> **Ex**. *Dame un **break** para arreglar mi **printer**, parece que no está funcionando.*

NOTE: English words that are used in Puerto Rico, but with a different spelling or usage than that common to English, or that are combined with Spanish words when used, are in the Spanish Lexicon section. Ex. *wiken* (weekend), *estoy relax* (I am hanging out or relaxed).

accurate	blue
anyway	boarding pass
barbecue (BBQ)	boyfriend
bike	break
black	brown
blister	bumper

cash	full (bed size)
cash flow	fun
cheeseburger	gay
chubby	gel
clear	girlfriend
closet	green
coffee break	grey
cool	grill
coolant	G-string
cover	hamburger
cranberry	handy man
crispy	happy
crunchy	happy hour
damn	hardware
e-mail	hicky
fast food	honeymoon
favor	hot dog
fifty-fifty	ketchup
freezer	king (bed size)
friendly	kinky
fruit salad	label

layout	refill
lipstick	roommate
mama's boy	sandwich
management	size
marketing	so
mattress	software
nasty	sorry
panty	spray
party	statement
penthouse	sticker
please	sure
plug (electrical outlet)	switch (on/off switch)
polite	tape
printer	taxes
puppy	ticket
queen (bed size)	tricky
rack	twin (bed size)
ready	whatever
realtor	yellow
record (medical chart)	yes

Lexicon: Puerto Rican & Slang Words

A

a billetazo limpio: obtain or achieve something with a large amount of money.

a como dé lugar: at any cost, strong or extreme desire to achieve something.

a curcur: continually, without breathing especially related to drinking.

★ **a dos por chavo**: 1. extremely cheap, a good bargain. 2. not worth much, poorly made. 3. common, easy to get a hold of.

a la cañona: full force, all out.

a la intemperie: outdoors.

★ **a la orden**: at your service.

a la soltá: from the beginning.

★ **a las millas**: extremely fast or haphazardly. *Ex. Hoy salí a* *las millas para llegar a la reunión a tiempo, pero dejé la presentación en casa.*

a lo que venimos: let's get to work; let's get started with the task at hand.

a mi plín: 1. who cares, it's not my business. 2. I told you so.

a nivel: a person did something properly or by the book, on the up and up.

a pulmón: with a lot of force, overcoming obstacles especially by oneself.

a pulso: to achieve something through hard work and persistence.

a to' fuete (a todo fuete): full steam ahead, advancing rapidly.

★ **a to' jender (a todo jender)**: 1. to go fast, 2. to have the volume (ex. music) turned up high.

a tuqui: (syn. *a tuquiti*) an exp. of surprise or admiration.

abombao: smelly, stinky.

abuchear: to boo or yell insults.

aburrido como una ostra: bored out of your mind, extremely bored.

acángana: word used to replicate the sound of something falling, hitting or running into something else.

acaramelado: sweet, romantic, lovey-dovey.

★ ◉ **acerola**: a Caribbean cherry, often used to make juice.

acicalao: cool, happening.

acumular puntos: to get in good with someone.

adentro: prison. *Ex. Por corrupto, lo metieron pa' dentro.*

¡Adios!: exclamation used to express surprise or strong disagreement.

aflojar: to pay up, loosen the purse strings.

afrentao (afrentado): a selfish person that wants everything for himself; a materialistic person.

agallao: to be angry with.

agua de azahar: home remedy for anxiety, a tranquilizer.

agua de piringa: a watered-down or tasteless drink.

agua negra: sewer water.

aguajero: a person that fakes or doesn't follow up with what he promises.

★ **aguantado**: held up, holding in, keeping quiet or reserved, not expressing one's opinion.

aguantar el pico: to reduce the amount of food consumed, literally "to control the beak."

aguántate!: calm down, relax, cool your jets.

aguita: the blame.

aguzar: to wise up, to wake up, to pay attention.

★ **ah pues bien**: sarcastic exp. for "Oh, great!", "fantastic", "wonderful".

ahí, en la lucha: "in the grind", fighting or struggling along.

ahí, tirando —"hanging around", responding to the question "What's up?"

• ahí, en la lucha

ahora sí que nos salvamos!: sarcastic form of saying "We're in trouble now" or "We're in for it now", "We're screwed."

★ **ahorita**: in a while, or a while ago. This is different from other Spanish speaking countries where this means "right away" and can cause confusion if the traveler is not familiar with the Puerto Rican usage.

🍽 **ajonjolí**: sesame seeds.

★ **ajorado**: in a hurry, rushed for time.

ajumarse, ajumado: to be buzzed or almost drunk.

al garete: out of control.

alcahuete: 1. someone that tries to please everyone, or do everything that someone asks for. 2. a gopher. 3. a kiss-up, a suck-up.

alcancía: butt crack.

★ ᛁ᧞ᛁ **alcapurrias**: a fried food made with plaintains and then stuffed with pork, beef, crab, etc.

aletear: to wiggle as a fish.

ᛁ᧞ᛁ **almojábana**: a typical Puerto Rican fried food made from rice.

altanero: with attitude.

alza la pata y lambe: a sarcastic response to someone that says he is hungry, literally means "raise your leg and lick."

★ ᛁ᧞ᛁ **amarillos**: (syn. *maduros*) a fried plantain side dish that is often served for both lunch and dinner.

amogollao: soggy food.

añangotarse: to squat.

anda pál sirete: "Damn!", "Shoot!", "Darn!", "Holy Cow!"

★ 💧 **anda pál cará (anda para el carajo)**: 1. damn, darn; used when you forget something or did something. 2. exp. to communicate surprise or disbelief.

andariego: someone that is in the street a lot, not at home. someone that goes out all the time.

añoñar: to spoil someone, to dote over.

★ **apagao (apagado)**: someone is turned off, shut off, completely quiet, reserved or lacks energy.

apear: to get down from or climb out from a vehicle.

apestillao: kissing, making out, stuck together.

aplatanao (aplatanado): lack of ambition, lazy, a loafer, a slacker.

apretar el paso: to accelerate something, to speed it up, literally "to squeeze the step."

apretujaos: to be caressing, hugging and kissing your partner.

aprontao (aprontado): someone that jumps ahead or advances without waiting for his proper turn.

apunta, pero no dispares: joking phrase used when some sticks their rear end in your face, literally "aim, but don't fire".

apuntarse el baño: to not bathe oneself for a day.

aquí están que cortan: a hostile environment, a place that could explode at any moment.

aquí hay gato encerrado: something fishy is going on, something's not right.

aquí tú ya no mojas: someone no longer has power or respect with someone or in a certain place.

★ ¡◉¡ **arañitas**: literally "little spiders", a typical Puerto Rican side dish made from plantains finely grated into small sticks that are then fried in bunches.

¡◉¡ **arepa**: this is a flour tortilla that is generally served fried, and can be stuffed with cheese. Arepas are originally from Venezuela but are common in Fajardo and parts of southern Puerto Rico.

◆ **aquí hay gato encerrado**

arisco: very shy, cautious.

arranca en fá: the starting point.

arranca p' allá: go away, don't bother me.

arrancao (arrancado): broke financially.

• **arrancao (arrancado)**

arrancarle el brazo: (syn. arráncale la mano) to accept an offer immediately, to take advantage of an extraordinary offer.

arrancarle la mano: see *arrancarle el brazo*.

arreglar cuentas: to clear things up.

arresmillao (arresmillado): laugh a lot.

arrimado: dependent on others, a freeloader.

arrollao (arrollado): left holding the bag, screwed, S-O-L, out of luck.

asombrado: surprised, shocked.

★🍽 **asopao**: a rice soup often containing chicken, seafood or some type of meat.

ataque de cuernos: an attack of jealousy.

atar cabos sueltos: to tie up loose ends.

★**ATH**: The Puerto Rican equivalent to ATM. ATH means *A Toda Hora*, at any hour. Although the term comes from a specific network of ATM machines, it is used generically.

atorrante: a bum.

atracar: to eat a lot and swallow it all at once, almost to the point of choking.

★**atúquiti**: (syn. *cataplún*) a word used to express surprise.

¡Ave María purísima!: exp. of worry, frustration or pain.

¡Ave María!: exp. used to for surprise, happiness, admiration.

★ **averiguao**: (syn. *presentao*) nosy.

★**¡Ay bendito!** -(syn. *ay virgen*) phrase used to express commiseration or sorrow upon learning of bad news.

★ **¡Ay Señor!**: an exp. of worry or resignation.

★**¡Ay Virgen!**: see *¡Ay bendito!*.

B

babearse: to fall in love.

★☺ **baby**: (syn. *bebé*) term of affection like my dear, honey or sweetie. *Ex. ¿Baby, puedes salir a comprar leche para el café?*

bache: mud.

bajar el moco: calm down, relax, take it easy.

bajarle (fuerte) a alguien: to put someone in their place, speaking rudely.

bajo mundo: the underworld, like the mafia, etc.

balneario: a public beach.

balompie: soccer.

barajiarla más despacio: literally "shuffle slower" but means to explain with more details.

baratillo: cheap, almost given away.

barrito: zit, pimple.

batata política: a political appointee that has his position because of friends and not because of competence.

🍽 **batida**: a milk shake.

bayú: a party among friends, a get together.

bebé: 1. see *baby*, 2. a baby.

bembé: a party.

★**bendito**: what a pity, poor thing.

★**bestial**: (syn. *brutal, está cañón*) good, great, wonderful, marvelous, fantastic, stupendous.

bibí: baby bottle.

👄*☺ **bicha**: bitch.

👄*☺ **bichería**: snobby, arrogant, act superior to others.

👄***bicho**: dick.

bichote: drug dealer.

bichoteado: laying low, reserved, not noticeable.

★ **bien bestial**: see *bien brutal*.

★**bien brutal**: fantastic, incredible, amazing. *Ex. Anoche el concierto fue <u>bien brutal</u>, cantaron casi 3 horas.*

bien y más: phrase used to highlight agreement with an action.

☺ **biles**: bills.

☺🍺 **birra**: beer.

★🍽 **bizcocho**: cake.

blanquito: whitey, a reference to a snobby, stuck up person.

★☺ **blower**: blow dryer.

bobo: 1. fool, 2. pacifier for a baby.

★ **bochinche**: a piece of gossip.

bochinchero/a: gossipy.

bochornoso, bochorno: shameful.

bodrogos: ugly, stinky or old shoes.

bombas y platillos: introduce something with a lot of fanfare, publicity or noise.

bombero/a: person that stands someone else up.

bondo: makeup.

boquete: 1. pothole. 2. a hole.

★**boquiabajo**: a jaw-dropping surprise.

★ **Boricua**: Puerto Rican, comes from the term used by the natives of Puerto Rico.

★ **Borinquen**: the Taino native indian term used for Puerto Rico.

borrón y cuenta nueva: a clean slate, to start from fresh.

botao como bolsa: someone that was thrown out abruptly, from a job or a relationship.

botar el verde de las tripas: to throw up excessively.

botar la bola: something extraordinary or extremely successful, comes from baseball and refers to "hitting a home run."

bragueta: zipper.

★☺ **breakecito**: a break, as in give me a break or give me a moment.

★ **bregar**: 1. to behave, 2. to work on, to deal with.

★☺ **breiquecito**: alt. sp. for *breakecito*.

brete: a love affair.

brillar por su ausencia: to call attention by not being present.

brincacharcos: pants that are too short in the legs.

★**brinco, brincar**: a jump, to jump, to jump on or attack someone.

★☺ **broder (brother)**: literally brother, but used like dude or man.

★ **brutal**: see *bestial*.

★**bruto**: a fool or idiot, see *sángano*.

💣☀☺ **bucha**: lesbian, butch.

buche: a taste of, a sip of, a mouthful of.

buchipluma: someone that does not do what he says, or does not keep his word.

★ **buen provecho**: Bon Appetit, said to others when beginning to eat, or when one enters a room or area where others are eating.

★ **buena gente**: a good person, literally "good people".

bueno/buenón/buenote: handsome, attractive.

buitre: a vulture; someone preying on others in a romantic sense.

buruquena: a river crab.

buscar cizañas: to create problems for others, blow things out of proportion.

buscar fuete para su fondillo: to do something prejudicial to oneself, having full knowledge of the consequences.

buscarle la vuelta a algo: to look for a solution to a problem.

buscón: a hustler, petty criminal.

C

caballo: a work horse, usually refers to a person that is very good or a master at what he does. *Ex. Eliseo es un caballo, vendiendo día y noche para llegar a la cuota,*

cabezudo: traditional Puerto Rican mask.

cachapera: lesbian.

caché: elegant, classy.

cachendoso: elegant, classy.

cachete: a freeby.

cachetero, cachetear: (syn. *jociador*) freeloader, to freeload, cheapskate.

caer en cuenta: to understand something that was previously not understand.

caerle como bomba: to not go over well, to not get along with (can be in reference to a person or to food).

• **Buscarle la vuelta a algo**

caerle la macacoa: to have something go wrong (in an economic sense).

caerse de la mata: to be obvious.

★ ♦ **cafre**: (syn. *charro*) refers to a person that uses many expletives, a person that dresses cheaply (like a prostitute), or a person that speaks in an uneducated form; it is an insult for someone to be called *cafre*.

♦ **cagar**: to shit.

♦ **cagar más arriba del culo**: spend beyond one's means, to appear better off economically than is really the case.

◦caerse de la mata

♦ **cagar más que un pato amarrao**: literally "to shit more than a tied duck."

♦ **cagarse en su madre**: literally "to shit on one's mother", to be pissed off at someone.

caí como pana: to fall out of grace, to lose everything you have worked hard for.

calentar los motores: to warm the engines, to get ready to start an activity.

calumnias, calumniar: lies, to tell lies about someone.

cambiar chinas por botellas: to come out on the losing end of an exchange.

• caerle como bomba

💣 **camón**: whore.

candela: the flame of a fire.

caneca: a type of bottle or jug.

cangrimán: a smooth operator, a slick person.

cañiña de mono: 1. curly hair. 2. an uphill struggle, something that is not easy.

★ **cantazo**: (syn. *guatapanazo*) a whoopin', a beating.

canto, cantito: a piece, a taste, a nibble or bit of something.

capear: to buy drugs.

cara larga: annoyed.

💣 **carajo**: 1. a far away place. 2. dammit.

carambola: a miracle.

carifresco: (syn. *caripelao*) shameless.

caripelao: see *carifresco*.

carreritas: the runs.

caserío: slum housing, public housing complexes that can sometimes be dangerous.

cataplún: see *atúquiti*.

centellazo: a whoopin'.

cereta: really curly hair.

cerrar con broche de oro: to end something on a high, on a good note, or to end a relationship on good terms.

cerrar el pico: literally "to shut the beak", to shut up, shut your trap.

cerveza negra: a sweet, malt-based non-alcoholic beverage.

chacho: derived from "muchacho", used to express relief or surprise.

chamba: luck or a fluke.

chambón: 1. large shoes. 2. a car clutch.

★☺ **chance**: a chance.

chanchullo: a scam, a trick, "pull strings" to achieve something.

chancleta: a sandal.

chancletero: a father whose children are all female.

chancro: (syn. *llaga*) scab.

changa, changuería: bothersome, but much less so than *majadera*, or even worse, *jodón*.

chango: 1. mischievous, coy, silly. 2. something tiny, puny or wimpy.

chao: goodbye, comes from the italian ciao.

chapucear, chapucero/a: to do something half ass or poorly.

charro: see *cafre*.

★ **chavar**: (syn. *jorobar*) to bug, bother, annoy.

★ **chavienda**: (syn. *jodienda, julepe*) annoying, bothersome.

★ **chavo, chavito**: money or change. *Ex. Préstame 25 chavos para comprar un chicle.*

cheche: the best.

chencha: a low quality, lowly.

cheque de goma: rubber check, bounced check.

☺ **chequear**: to check.

★ **chévere**: cool.

💣 **chichar**: to fuck.

chillar goma: to burn rubber, squeal tires.

chillo/a, chillito/a: lover. *Ex. Aunque él es casado, siempre tiene una chilla por allí.*

chillón: a loud or distracting color or noise.

★🍽 **china**: an orange (the fruit). *Ex. Pásame el jugo de china, por favor.*

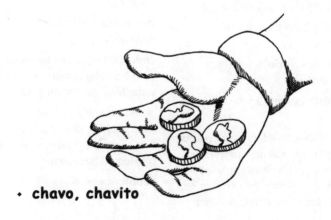

• **chavo, chavito**

chinche: a lot of something all at once or all of a sudden.

chinchorro: a run-down or poorly kept building.

chingo: a mutt.

chino: intentional rub or contact with the frontal portion of one person's waist against the rear end of another person, has a sexual connotation.

chipichapi: something of poor quality or cheap.

☺ **chipy**: something cheap, but in a negative sense.

chiquitín: someone small or tiny.

chiringa: kite.

chiripa: a small task or job.

chispito: a bit, a tad of something.

chiste colorado: a dirty or sexual joke.

chiste mongo: a joke that's not funny.

★ **chivo**: 1. refers to the part of a job that was not completely finished. Ex. Washing a car but missing a part; the part that was missed is the *chivo*. Another

example is when a woman shaves her legs but misses a portion; the hairy portion she missed is the *chivo*. 2. a side job, something extra to bring in a little money 3. a fluke or lucky shot.

chivo loco: someone crazy.

💣 **chocha**: pussy.

chola: head.

choreto: a lot of something.

chorro: a stream of something, a lot of something to the point of overabundance.

chotear: to snitch or inform on someone.

chucha: the blank tile in dominoes.

chuchería: something insignificant.

chuchín: term of endearment used between couples, means something yummy or good.

★ **chulería**: (syn. *chulin, chulisnaquin, chulo*) a sweet, nice or caring person, someone pleasant to be around.

chulin: see *chulería*.

chulisnaquin: see *chulería*.

★ **chulo**: see *chulería*.

💣 **chulo 'e puta (chulo de puta)**: pimp, a guy that manages prostitutes.

chumbo/a: a flat rear end, no curves.

☺ **chunquear**: to barf, especially in reference to being drunk.

chupárselo: to accept or swallow something against one's wishes; to bite your tongue.

💣 **churra**: the runs, or shit.

💣 **churretiá (churretiada)**: shit.

chuz: correct, fine, elegant.

🍴 **ciento en boca**: a type of cookie.

cizañero: a trouble-maker.

☺ **cloche**: clutch.

coco: a head, especially a bald one.

cocolo: salsa music lover.

cocotazo: rap on the head (for kids) as punishment.

★ **coger**: grab, pick up, take, run into (a traffic jam). This word does not have the same expletive meaning that is true for other Latin American countries.

coger calle: to go out a lot.

coger de punto: to choose a person to be the brunt of the joke.

coger fiao: to take something without immediately paying, but paying later.

coger la juyilanga: to party.

coger pon: to hitch hike or catch a ride.

coger por el cuello: to castigate, wring someone's neck.

coger todo a pecho: to take everything to heart, take things too seriously.

cogerle repelillo: to have a bad taste of (food, drinks, etc.), something you tried and don't want to have anything to do with.

cogerlo con pinzas: to be very cautious or careful, literally "to grab it with tweezers."

cogerlo de mangó bajito: (syn. *cogerlo de zuruma*) to take advantage of someone.

cogerlo de zuruma: see *cogerlo de mangó bajito*.

cogerse bien: to fit in, to get along with.

cogerse en un dos por tres: quickly, right away.

cogérsela larga: to stay out all night.

cohítre: a type of weed found in Puerto Rico.

colarse: to butt in line.

colegio: a private school, as opposed to an *escuela* which is a public school.

colgado: failed at school.

colgarse: to fail a class.

collera: a bum, vulgar or mean-spirited person.

colmar la copa: to be fed up.

colmo: the worst.

comadre: literally the godmother of your child but often used to mean a really close person to your family, a best friend.

★ **comay**: sl. for *comadre*.

★ **comemierda**: (syn. *parejero*) a snobby person who is presumptuous and believes to be above others, often used in reference to social or economic class; literally "shit eater."

comegofio: a screw-off, someone that wastes time.

comer arroz con perico: to speak incessantly.

comer banco: warm the bench (in reference to sports).

comer jobos: to cut class, to skip school.

comer la vista: colors or designs so outlandish or bright that they block the vision.

comer más que una llaga mala: to eat excessively.

comerle los dulces: to beat someone at his own game.

comerse el pare: to run through a stop sign.

comerse la luz: to run a red light.

comerse un cable: to be bored.

comiste chuletas plásticas: sarcastic phrase used to tell someone that they are blocking one's vision; "you make a better door than window."

como congo de jolla: drunk.

como cucaracha en baile de gallina: out of place.

como el cangrejo, siempre para atrás: a loser, someone that does nothing with his life.

como el rabo del perro... atrás: being the last, as in the dog's tail.

¿Cómo es la cosa?: What's going on?, What's happening here?

como gato que no va pá lejos: someone that doesn't progress or have a future.

como guineo en boca de vieja: to pass easily without force.

como la langosta: something with a large tail/rear-end; literally "like a lobster."

como nalga de bebé: literally "like a baby's bottom", very soft.

como tres en un zapato y yo en el medio: someone just scraping by, just surviving with what they earn.

compadre: literally the godfather of your child but often used to mean a really close person to your family.

compay: 1. sl. for *compadre*, a close friend. 2. godfather.

con el hoy y con el mañana: justification for not having done something.

¿Con esa moneda me pagas?: This is how you repay me?,

• **como guineo en boca de vieja**

phrase used to express disgust with how one is being treated after doing something helpful for the other person.

con tu permiso, dijo Monchito: exp. used to excuse oneself for an interruption.

★**condenado**: literally "condemned", damned, darned.

conejillo de India: a guinea pig; a person used as a test subject.

confianzú: a freeloader, someone that takes advantage of the hospitality that is extended to him.

coño: damn.

contra viento y marea: fighting or struggling against all odds, paddling against the current.

contrallao (contrallado): someone set in their ways, pig-headed.

☺ **cooleado, coolear**: cool, relaxed, reserved.

★ **coquí**: a small tree frog typical in Puerto Rico; its grasshopper-sounding chirp can be heard generally in the evening; this frog is the unofficial mascot of Puerto Rico.

🍽 **coquito**: an egg nog-like drink served during the Christmas holidays (generally contains alcohol).

★ **coraje**: anger.

corillo: group of friends.

correr bike: to ride a bike.

correr como yegua esnúa: literally "to run like a naked mare", to run swiftly.

correr la máquina: to fool someone into saying or doing something that he was not planning on doing.

cortarse las venas: to be in love to the point of committing suicide, *a la* Romeo and Juliet.

corte de pastelillo: to cut off someone while driving.

cortos: shorts.

cotorra: a talking bird, parrot.

coyera: alt. sp. of *collera*.

☺ **crayola**: a crayon, based on the brand of crayons "Crayola", but used generically.

creer que se tiene a Dios agarrado por el rabo: to believe oneself owner of the absolute truth.

crestú no, gallo bolo: joking phrase used in response to the question "*Qué crees tú?*"

☙ **crica**: pussy.

☙ **crical**: the strong form of *revolú*.

criollo: native to Puerto Rico (in reference to people or things, especially food).

crispy: 1. pissed, annoyed, angry. 2. an Afro or curly hair.

cruu: raw, as in food.

cruzar el charco: to travel to the United States mainland.

cuadrarse: to confront someone, with attitude.

cuajar: literally "to coagulate", but often used to mean give it more time, let it alone for a little longer, etc.

🍽 **cuajito**: pig's intestinal wall, to eat.

cualquier cosa: a phrase meaning "whatever you need" or "anything you need."

cuando Colón baje el dedo: never, when pigs fly.

¿Cuándo más?: when else? used sarcastically.

cuatro: a type of guitar with only four strings. For this reason it is named the *cuatro* or four in Spanish.

cúcame, Pedro, que a mí me gusta: phrase to reprimand someone that is teasing or making fun of another.

cucar: to provoke.

cucarachero/a: a penny-pincher, thrifty to the point of exaggeration.

🍽 **cucas**: a type of hard cracker.

cucas monas: (syn. *muecas*) faces made, especially at a baby.

🍽 **cuchifrito**: anything fried in batter.

cuchucientas veces: thousands of times, a ton, infinite times.

cuco: the Boogie Man.

cuero: prostitute or easy woman.

cuesta arriba: difficult.

cuesta un ojo de la cara: cost an arm and a leg, literally "costs one eye of the face."

cuica: a jump rope.

culeco/a: 1. happy, content for achieving something. 2. An excited or stimulated person (can be romantically but not necessarily).

culipandear: to waste time or mess around.

curarse en salud: to play it safe.

D

dale clóset: (syn. *dale gancho, dale percha*) used when someone uses an article of clothing too much, literally means give it to the closet.

dale gancho: literally "give it a hanger", see *dale clóset*.

dale percha: see *dale clóset*.

dale un fajazo: to ask someone for money.

dame la vuelta: phrase used when someone is called the wrong name.

dame un la: give me a clue or a hint.

dar bandazos: to fall asleep.

dar candela: to bother, nag.

dar coba: to make envious.

dar cráneo: to think or consider something deeply, to give thought to.

dar el mameyazo fatal: to give the fatal blow, the *coup-de-grace*.

dar en el clavo: to hit the nail on the head.

dar la cara: to assume responsibility for something.

dar lata: to talk a lot, without saying anything.

dar pachó: to feel embarrased, to go through an embarrassing situation.

★☺ **dar un break**: to give someone a break, an opportunity or chance.

dar un chin: to give a little bit.

★ **dar un coraje**: to anger.

dar una orejita: to give a hint.

darle cabulla: to let someone loose, to see where they end up.

darle color a algo: to assign something more importance than it deserves.

darle un toque: to give something a nudge to get it moving forward again.

darse la vuelta: to not compare someone with another person, if the first person does not like the second.

★ **darse un palo**: to have a drink, especially alcoholic.

darse una matá (matada): 1. to kill oneself doing something; *Ex. El se dio una matá ayer terminando el trabajo antes de irse de vacaciones.* 2. to fall down.

de a vicio: having too much of something.

de cachete: for free.

de chamba: luckily.

de cuello blanco: white collar.

de eso nada, monada, y de lo otro, cero: No!, No way!, Hell no!

de Guatemala a guatapeor: exp. meaning from bad to worse.

💣 **de mi maíz ni un grano**: a crude way to say that someone will not be privilege to one's sexual favors.

de paquete: new, straight from the wrapper, straight from the package.

de pura cepa: a native of somewhere, pure bred.

de rabo a cabo: to look for something high and low.

dejar algo a medio palo: without end.

dejar arrollao a alguien: to stand up, to miss a meeting.

dejar plantado: to stand someone up.

dejar sobre el tapete: to leave pending.

dejarlo: to leave it, forget it, drop it.

★ **del país**: locally made/grown as in vegetables.

del tingo al tango: from one to the other, back and forth.

desbaratada, desbaratar: worn out.

descará (descarada): "with what right", "where do you get off".

★ **desmadre**: (syn. *despelote*) a mess, a disaster, a situation out of control.

despabilao: distracted, in a trance.

★ **despelote**: see *desmadre*.

despojar: to take off or remove something from oneself.

desto: a contraction for the phrase de esto, from that.

☺ **diez cuatro**: 10-4, understood.

dímelo cantando: tell me everything, don't hold anything back.

dispararse la maroma: (syn. *tirarse la maroma*) to risk doing something.

★**disparate**: something that doesn't make sense or is out of context, *una locura*.

donde se resbala este, se escocota un mono: keen, streetwise, knows the ropes.

droguita: cheat sheet.

☺ **dron**: trashcan, probably from the word drum (as in barrel).

☺ **dropearse**: to drop out or quit (from a class or school).

E

★ **¡ea diache!**: exp. of surprise, Gee!, Wow!

¡ea rayo!: exp. to communicate surprise.

echa pa acá: come here.

echa pa allá: leave, get out of here.

echar chispas: to be pissed off.

echar flores: to flatter or shower with complements.

★ **echar p'alante**: to fight on, to move on, to progress.

echar un pie: to dance.

💣 **echar una criolla**: to shit.

echarle el ojo: to keep an eye on.

echarle fli: to dump a boyfriend or girlfriend.

echarle las cacas a alguien: to blame someone.

echarse para atrás: to back off from a decision especially at the last minute.

echársela: to complement oneself even to the point of vanity.

echón, echona: a show-off, a vain person, someone with a large ego.

Eeejeee!: exp. like Woowho!!

el bofe ahoga: something easy to do or get.

el cuento del pescaíto: a ruse, a lie.

él es una dama: a nice man, a very easy-going person, a great guy.

el gordo: the lottery.

embalao (embalado): in a hurry.

embarazada: pregnant (for an animal).

embeleco: 1. quickfix, duct tape type fix, 2. invent something.

embollao: mixed up with someone (in a relationship).

embrollao: mixed up in (debt or problems).

emburujao (emburujado): a mixed-up, unclear situation, snafu.

★ **embuste**: 1. a lie, 2. "I don't believe you."

embustero: a liar, to pull someone's leg.

empachao: fed up with.

empachar: to be stuffed or to have an upset stomach.

empaquetar: to sell someone a bill of goods.

empatar la pelea: to make ends meet.

empatar la pelea

emperifollao (emperifollado): lots of jewelry or accessories.

en dos patadas: quickly.

en el año de las guácaras: a long, long time ago.

en el baúl: (syn. *metido en el baúl*) when someone is controlled by another person; "Eating out of the palm of one's hand."

en la brega: working to get by, in the grind; similar to *en la lucha*.

en la lucha: literally "in the struggle" but is closer to "in the grind" referring to work or a job.

en lo que el hacha va y viene: to take advantage of time while waiting that something happens.

en sus lenguas quedo: phrase to say goodbye, means that now that one is leaving the others can gossip about him or her.

en un dos por tres: something easy to do.

★ **enamorao**: (syn. *mujeriego*) a womanizer.

eñangotao (eñangotado): squatting, alt. sp. of *añangotao*.

encabuya y vuelve y tira: repeat an action to see if you have better luck.

encharcao: soaking wet.

enchismao (enchismado): pissed off, annoyed, mad at.

enchismarse: to be bothered by.

★**enchulao (enchulado), enchularse**: madly in love with.

enchumbao (enchumbado): soaked, generally from rain, or being submerged in water.

encontronazo: a confrontation, a clash.

eñemao: dead tired.

enfiebrao (enfiebrado): crazy about something.

★ **enfogonao (enfogonado)**: very angry, pissed off.

enfuscar: to fall in love, to be distracted by love.

engatusar: to get caught up in, to get sucked into something (crime, fraud, etc).

engreído: rotten, vain, stuck up, arrogant.

enmonguillao (enmonguillado): come down with a cold, comes from having the *monga*.

ensalchichao (ensalchichado): people squished together, like sardines; literally "sausaged" together.

entrar en el combo: to be accepted into the group.

entrar por arrimao y salir por dueño: to arrive or start with nothing and now have everything.

entre la espada y la pared: a no win situation, between a rock and a hard place.

entripao: soaked, wet.

★ **entrometío (entrometido)**: see *averiguao*.

envellonao: annoyed, pissed.

equelecuá: okay.

equis o ye: this or that, for whatever.

eres como el cohítre: a resilient person, a survivor, someone that always pulls through.

ernú: an alternate pronunciation of *esnú*.

es el hace, el hace tiempo: a has-been, someone that is getting old.

es tan duro que se come la ropa vieja: cheap, selfish, greedy.

esas son palabras con luz: phrase used when someone says something obvious.

escamado: scared, nervous, paranoid.

escampar: to stop raining.

escocotar: to beat up or injure, to fall down and injure oneself.

☺ **escrin**: a screen (computer or window).

escudriñao: to investigate.

escuela: a public school, as opposed to a *colegio*, which is a private school.

ese es de clavo pasado: a diehard, a fanatic, to the core.

ese es de tierra adentro: a hillbilly, a mountain person.

ese es otro cantar: that's not what was heard, that's different from what I understood.

ese perro me mordió: literally "that dog bit me", exp. used to communicate that the information that is being told to someone is already known by that person.

ese tiene ínfulas de grandeza: a snob, someone that is stuck on himself, images of grandeur.

esguañangao: tired, exhausted.

eslapao: to have a flat or skinny stomach.

eslembao (eslembao): surprised or in limbo.

esmallao: hungry for something (used not only for food.

esnú: naked, slang for the word *desnudo*.

★ **eso es así**: darn tootin', damn straight, that's it all right, ain't that right, you got that right.

eso es como predicar en el desierto: it's like talking to a wall.

eso es de cariño: phrase just kidding, it was a joke.

eso es lo que trajo el barco: literally "that is what the boat brought", meaning that's all there is, take it or leave it.

★ **eso está filete**: see *quitado*.

eso hace orilla: a lot of something, overflowing.

eso ni me va ni me viene: to not care about something one way or the other.

eso se cae de la mata: something obvious.

eso trae cola: have consequences, this is not the end of the matter.

★ **esos son otros veinte pesos**: "that's a whole different story."

espacharrao (espacharrado): smash into pieces, flatten, mash.

●゙ **espatarrá (espatarrada)**: with open legs, spread eagle; may be used sexually.

★ **espejuelos**: eye glasses.

☺ **espotear**: to put oneself in the spotlight, to stand out.

esta atrás y no avanza: someone that has fallen behind in work, someone not living up to standards.

★ **está cañón**: see *bestial*.

está de calle: something good enough to sell.

★ **está fuerte**: 1. to cross the line, to say or do something out of place, 2. to be a lot of work within the given time.

está to' hablao (está todo hablado): everything already agreed upon, or discussed.

esta X: to be cool, amazing, happening.

están cortados con la misma tijera: made from the same cloth, like father like son.

están que truenan: mad, annoyed, pissed off.

estar a ley de: about to achieve or complete something.

estar acabando: to be successful this moment (either in your career or with women).

estar adobao: to be excessively sweaty.

★ **estar al palo**: fashionable, the "in" thing.

estar alzao: to be furious, mad, bothered.

estar aniao: to live permanently with someone, comes from *estar anillado* (to be ringed).

estar arresmillao: to laugh to the point that your teeth are showing.

estar bisorioco: to be defectuous.

estar blindao: to be extremely well prepared.

estar bregao: to be well dressed, matching.

★ 💣 **estar cabrón**: 1. to be a complicated or screwed up situation, 2. to be incredible, wonderful, amazing (in a positive sense).

💣 **estar caliente**: 1. to be in trouble for causing problems for someone else. *Ex. Este tipo está caliente porque le chocó el carro al papá.* 2. to be horny.

estar choreto: a lot of something, overflowing, abundant, large quantities.

estar cocinando algo: to be cooking something up, to be planning something in secret.

estar como coco: top physical shape.

estar como el hilo 80: 1. thin, 2. without money, penniless.

estar como el jamón de sandwich: (syn. *ser como el jamón de sandwich*) to be stuck in the middle of two opposing sides, to be mixed up in a problem or mess.

estar como un cañón: someone healthy, in good shape, strong.

estar de boya: to be in good humor.

estar de carreritas: to have diarrea.

estar de magazine: to be very pretty or elegant, to be done up as if in a magazine.

estar de vaca: to be on vacation.

★**estar del carajo**: to be unsupportable.

★ **estar del caray**: (syn. *estar del mero*) to step out of line with something, to go overboard.

estar del mero: see *estar del caray*.

estar embarrao: to be fearful.

estar emborujao: to be wrapped up or mixed up in.

estar embrollao: to be up to your eyes in debt.

estar emburujá: to be wrapped up in something (ex. the sheets in bed).

estar empancinao: extremely full, to the point of exploding.

estar empaquetao: more formally dressed than the occasion merits, dressed to the nines.

estar empataos: to be boyfriend and girlfriend, to be a pair or a couple.

estar en el guiso: to be in an advantageous position in relation to a potential job.

estar en el mambo: to be in the middle of what's happening.

estar en issue: to be in discussion.

estar en las papas: to be well off, financially.

estar en pañales: literally "in diapers", still learning the ropes, just getting started.

estar en territorio apache: enemy territory or a very dangerous area.

estar en tiempo muerto: down time, period of little work.

estar enchumbao: to be soaking wet.

estar enfogonao: to be mad or pissed off.

estar entera: 1. to be hot, good looking (sexually).

estar entregao: completely focused on something.

estar esmangaletiá: poorly dressed, disheveled.

estar esmayao: to be starving.

estar espaciao (espaciado): spaced out.

★ **estar fajao**: working hard to finish something, break one's back working.

estar forrao de chavos: to have a lot of money.

☺ **estar frizao**: to be frozen or stuck.

estar guisando: to not do much and earn a lot of money.

estar haciéndose: to fake or pretend.

☺ **estar haciéndose pipi**: to urinate.

estar hasta los lerenes: to be fed up with or tired of something.

estar hecho leña: to be worn out, tired, sore.

estar jendío: extremely drunk.

estar más perdío que un juey bizco: to be lost, confused or disoriented.

estar pasado: to step over the line.

★ **estar pelao**: financially broke.

estar planchado: 1. done, finished, agreed upon. 2. easy.

estar por el libro: in perfect condition.

estar pugilateao: frustrated, bothered, preoccupied or nervous.

estar que no hay quien le beba el caldo: to be in bad humor.

☺ **estar relax**: to be relaxed.

estar tapao: blocked up, in reference to constipation.

estar tirao: poorly dressed.

☺ **estartear**: to start something, as in a car engine.

estirar la pata: to die or pass away.

estracijao (estracijado): poorly dressed.

estrafalario: a disorganized, disheveled, unclean person, a bum or vagrant.

★ **estrésico/a**: stressed.

★ **explotá (explotada)**: tired, worn out, wasted.

F

fajao: focused on a job, working hard.

fajaso: trying to get something for free, or borrowing something without the intention of paying it back.

fajón: good or capable, generally used in reference to a hard worker.

faltarle un tornillo: to have a screw loose, to be crazy.

💣 **farifo/a**: gay or lesbian.

★☺ **faxear**: to fax.

feliz como lombriz: happy as a clam, literally "happy as an earthworm."

feto: an ugly or comely person.

fichu: (syn. *firulistica*) very fashionable, dressed up.

fiebrar: to do the "in" thing.

fiebrú: fan, fanatic, enthusiast

fino: good, "fine."

firulistica: see *fichu*.

fisna: dainty.

☺ **fixear**: to fix something.

☺ **flama**: a flame.

· **feliz como lombriz**

flechao (flechado): literally "arrowed" from Cupid's bow, in love.

💣 **fleje**: a prostitute, an easy or slutty person.

☺ **flushear**: to flush the toilet.

fó: yuck (for food or anything else) in relation to its smell.

fochi: yuck (for food or anything else), gross.

fofo: flabby, out of shape.

fonda: an inexpensive place to eat, generally typical Puerto Rican food.

★ **fondillo**: heiny, rear-end.

fondita: a local café or restaurant where typical Puerto Rican fare is served.

fotuto: thing-a-ma-jig.

fracatán: a lot, a large amount or quantity.

• **flechao**

★ **frappé**: a drink similar to a daiquiri or piña colada but without the alcohol, generally made from fruit.

★ **fregadero**: sink.

fresco: fresh.

friendo y comiendo: right away, in a jiffy.

frío pelú: really cold, freezing.

frisa: a blanket.

☺ **frizarse**: to freeze up or get stuck.

fuácata: sound used to signify a crash.

fufú: a curse, a spell.

★ **fulano (de tal)**: (syn. *mengano, sultano, perencejo*) Joe Blow.

fumón: a wedgy.

funfuñoso: difficult, hard to please.

fututear: throw away, waste money.

G

gagear: to stutter.

gajes del oficio: things that happen, a part of life.

gallera: a cock-fighting ring.

‣ **friendo y comiendo**

★ ◉ **gandules**: peas; the correct spanish word is *gandures* but in Puerto Rico because of the sometimes unique pronunciation of the R sound, it is more often than not changed to L.

★ ☺ **ganga**: 1. a deal, offer, a steal, 2. a gang.

ganso: clever.

gatillero: a gun-for-hire, an assassin.

gato encerrao: something suspicious.

gistro: G-string.

◉ **gofio**: a powdered, sugared candy with brown sugar.

💣 **golfa**: whore or slut.

gozar un montón: to have a good time.

★ **grajear**: to smooch, suck face or make out.

greña: messed up hair, hair that stands up or is out of control.

★ **greñú**: (syn. *pelú*) hairy, lots of hair on the body.

★ **guagua**: bus, small truck, van.

guallar: to grate.

guame: (syn. *miqueo*) something easy, a piece of cake.

◉ **guanábana**: a soursop fruit.

guaraguao: a type of bird.

◉ **guarapo**: a juice made from sugarcane.

guardia: refers to any type of police officer or guard.

💣 **guardia palito**: literally "night stick guard" but refers to a rent-a-cop. This word is offensive for the person to whom it refers.

guasa: (syn. *guasimilla*) bull, nonsense, rubbish.

guasimilla: see *guasa*.

• **greña**

guatapanazo: see *cantazo*.

gufeao: cool.

guillú, guillado: vain, proud; to sneak something in front of people, like chocolate, etc.

guindalejos: decorations or things that hang from something else.

★🍽 **guineo**: banana.

güiro: a musical instrument; a hollow gourd stroked by a multi-fingered wire instrument.

guisito: a good thing, easy money.

hablando de todo un poco: phrase used to change subjects in or redirect a conversation.

hablando del Rey de Roma y las narices que se asoman: speak of the devil.

hablar baba: to babble, talk nonsense.

hablar fino: to speak properly or with eloquence.

hablar hasta por los codos: a person so talkative that he is boring and turns others off.

hablar más que una vieja sin tabaco: someone that talks too much.

H

ha llovido mucho: phrase used to express the passing of time, a long time ago.

haber gato en saco: means that there's a hidden or secret reason in what is being discussed.

★🍽 **habichuelas**: 1. beans, 2. means of living or sustenance, livelihood, "bread and butter".

• **haber gato en saco**

💣 **hablar mierda**: 1. to talk lies, literally "talk shit", 2. talk about trivial matters, to talk without saying anything important.

hablar paja: a mild form of *hablar mierda*.

hablar pestes: to speak badly of someone.

hablar raspao: to say something cleary or directly but rudely and impolitely.

hacer aguaje: a hollow threat.

hacer algo con las patas: doing something poorly or incorrectly.

hacer caso omiso: to ignore.

hacer cucas monas: to make goofy faces.

hacer escante: to make a mess.

hacer las paces: to ask for forgiveness, to excuse oneself.

hacer mofa, mofarse: to make fun of someone.

💣 **hacer posición cuatro**: 1. from ballet, to test drunks, 2. sexually doggy style.

hacer su agosto: to earn lots of money in a specific job that you did.

hacer un levante: to pick someone up, romantically.

hacer un serrucho: see *serrucho*.

hacerse de la vista larga: to ignore something or someone.

hacerse harina: to have an intimate encounter with someone, either for good or bad, romantically or fighting.

💣 **hacerse la casqueta**: to masturbate.

💣 **hacerse un polvito**: to jerk off.

hasta aquí me trajo el río: means that your patience has run out or that you have tried to resolve a situation every way possible without success.

hasta el cabo: until the job is done, until the end.

hasta el cogote: to be fed up with or tired of something.

hasta el copete: fed up with, annoyed with.

hasta el ñú: something went all the way in.

hasta la amanezca: until the sun comes up.

hasta la coronilla: fed up with, annoyed with.

hay cuatro gatos: a small amount of people, few people in a place (bar).

★ **heavy**: happening, cool.

hecho y derecho: 1. by the book, 2. finished!, done!

★☺ **hello**: duh. *Ex. Hello, ya hablamos de eso ayer, tonto!*

★💣 **hijo de puta**: son of a bitch.

💣 **hijo de tu madre**: son of a bitch.

☺ **horas pico**: peak hours.

huevo sin sal: a bitter person.

ir bumper con bumper: to tailgate someone.

★ **irse a pique**: to go bankrupt.

irse al baño: to get out of here, leave, screw off.

irse al mambo: to get down to business.

irse como pan caliente: to sell (out) something quickly.

irse de culo diciendo que no: to deny something emphatically.

irse de güira: to get something very easily.

irse hasta atrás: drunk.

I

idiotizado: idiotized, to become stupid.

importar un bledo: (syn. *importar un comino, importar un pepino*) to not care, not be interested, Who cares?

importar un comino: see *importar un bledo*.

importar un pepino: see *importar un bledo*.

• **irse como pan caliente**

J

jaiba: a wiseaker, a wise-ass.

jalar pata: to walk a lot.

jalda arriba: in spite of the obstacles.

jaleo: a growl from the stomach (for not having eaten).

jaletreo: a difficult person.

🍴 **jama**: food.

jamaquear: to shake or swing something from side to side.

jamás de los jamases: never ever, not in a million years.

jamona: old maid.

☺ **jangover**: hangover.

jangueado: hung or tied up; the phone lines are occupied, calls can't get through.

★☺ **janguear**: to hang out.

jaqueca: a hangover.

jarana: party, fiesta.

jartito: gorged with food, be extremely full.

jarto: fed up with something or someone.

★ **jebo/a**: sl. for a boyfriend or girlfriend; alt. sp. of *jevo/a*.

jenderse: drunk.

jendi'o: drunk.

jeringar: to bug, bother.

★ **jevo/a**: sl. for a boyfriend or girlfriend; alt. sp. of *jebo/a*.

★ **jíbaro/a**: originally refers to a person from the interior or mountains of Puerto Rico but has come to mean a hick or country bumkin. While the term can be used in a negative sense, many people are proud of being labeled *jíbaro*.

jimiquiar: to sob.

jincho: lilly white, pale.

jociador, jociar: see *cachetero*.

jockey: mens' underwear.

★💣 **joder**: to fuck or to fuck around with, to bother, to annoy.

💣 **jodienda**: (syn. *chavienda*) a mess, a screw up, a fuck up.

💣 **jodío**: screwed up, fucked up.

💣 **jodón**: annoying to the point of pissing someone off.

jolgorio: a party.

☺ **jonrón**: home run, from baseball, but also may be used in a literary sense.

jorobar: see *chavar*.

joseador: an opportunist.

★ **Juan del Pueblo**: Joe Blow.

juanetazo: alcoholic beverage or drink.

🍽 **jueyes**: crabs.

jugar bolita y hoyo con alguien: to know someone from childhood, to be extremely familiar with someone.

jugar dos bases: to cheat on or be unfaithful to someone.

jugar hasta la cota: to bet everything.

julepe: see *chavienda*.

jullilanga: a party.

jumeta: drunk.

juntos, pero no revueltos: to be with someone from necessity but not because of friendship or respect.

☺ **juqueado**: enthused, hooked, concentrated.

jurutungu: far away, in the middle of no where.

juyó: alternate form of saying *huyó*, ran away or escaped.

· **jonrón**

K

☺ **kinky**: 1. curly or knotted hair. 2. sexually deviant.

L

☝ **la cagó**: to have fucked up.

la calle está dura: it is difficult to find a job or to earn a living.

la fiesta del sorrullo, cada cual trae el suyo: BYOB, bring your own whatever to the party.

La Gobe: short for *La Gobernadora*, a reference to Puerto Rico's governor Sila Calderón.

la idea por la vuelta: to come and go quickly, to not dilly-dally.

la Inter: a reference to the Interamerican University.

★ **la isla**: any place outside of San Juan. *Ex. Vamos a la isla este fin de semana, para escaparnos de San Juan.*

la mandá se oyó en Nueva York: to tell someone off, to (figuratively) scream and yell about something.

la mató porque la quería: literally "he killed her because he loved her", sarcastic phrase used to explain when someone kills someone else.

la piña esta agria: poor situation economically, things are not going well, the economy is weak.

la sangre llama: literally "blood calls", refers to a person's feelings to go back to his roots and his family.

la seca y la meca: to visit everywhere in a short time.

★ **la UP**: pronounced *Yupi*; this is a reference to the University of Puerto Rico, but can specifically refer to the Río Piedras, San Juan campus.

ladies: the bathroom. *Ex. Dame un minuto para ir al ladies, antes de salir.*

lambío: a glutten, greedy selfish.

lambiscón: a "parasite" living off another person.

lameojo/lambeojo: brown-noser, someone that kisses up to the boss, etc.

lapa: 1. a person that is clingy, clingy, 2. freeloader.

lapachar: in a downpour, kids playing and jumping in the puddles, splashing around.

lares: places.

le comieron las tapas: they ate him up, they had him for breakfast.

le dieron como a pillo de película: (syn. *le dieron hasta por dentro del pelo, le dieron de arroz y de masa*) literally "they gave it to him like a robber in movies," they beat him badly.

le dieron de arroz y de masa: to be badly beaten in any type of competition, see *le dieron como a pillo de película*.

le dieron hasta por dentro del pelo: literally "they gave it to him even inside his hair", see *le dieron como a pillo de película*.

le dieron uno de cal y otro de arena: to receive good and bad news at the same time.

le importa un pirulí: to not care a bit.

le ronca la manigueta: to be bothered by someone, to get someone's goat by teasing him.

le sacaron el dinero con alicate: means that someone is extremely stingy or tight with money.

leche: luck.

lechú: a lucky-duck, a lucky person.

lenguetera: a gossip.

lenguilarga: a gossip or someone that exaggerates and embellishes stories, talkative.

◆ le sacaron el dinero con alicate

levantar una roncha: to start a fight, confrontation or argument.

💣 **¡lezna!**: exp. (syn. *lezna es*) Forget it!, Buzz off!, Show off!

💣 **¡lezna es!**: see *lezna*.

librar la coca: to end a losing streak.

liga: a mix of something.

ligar: 1. to ogle or gawk at, in a sexual sense, 2. to mix, 3. to spie on.

limazo: a reprimand or scolding.

limpiarle la cacharra: to kill off.

☺ **liquear**: to leak. *Ex. Después de la tormenta, el techo de mi casa estaba liqueando*.

llaga: see *chancro*.

★ **llamar para atrás**: literally "to call back."

llevar la voz cantante: to lead a group, to grab the reins.

llevarse hasta los clavos de la cruz: to rob blind.

llover sobre mojao: to cry over spilt milk.

lo dices y no lo sabes: you can say that again.

lo mismo raspa que pinta: a person that has extensive abilities, a jack-of-all-trades.

lo pasaron por la piedra: to be strongly reprimanded, or to be abused.

lo puso a sudar la gota gorda: to pass through a hard, difficult or uncomfortable situation.

lo puso como chupa de china: to reprimand, confront or chastise someone.

lo puso en un tres y dos: to put someone in a confusing, uncertain position.

lo que le salga de los pantalones: whatever he wants to do is his choice, he's big enough to make his own decisions.

lo salvó la campana: saved by the bell.

lo tuyo viene: yours is coming.

lo último en la avenida: the latest thing, the current fad or fashion.

loco: dude, man.

loquera: craziness, crazy, wild, nutty.

los huevos se van a poner a peso: the economic situation of someone is getting tight or worse.

los kioskos: reference to a series of kiosks along the highway in Luquillo, Puerto Rico. These kiosks sell all variety of local Puerto Rican cuisine, especially fried foods. They are a typical stop on the way between San Juan and Fajardo, San Juan and El Yunque, or as a destination for a day trip on the island.

❧ **los niños hablan cuando las gallinas mean**: children should be seen and not heard.

lucirse chayote: to cross the line.

M

maceta: cheap.

☺ **machina**: literally "a machine".

machua: a manly looking woman.

🍽 **maduros**: see *amarillos*.

★ **mahón**: jeans.

mai: ma, mommy.

★🍽 **majada**: mashed, often in reference to potatoes.

majadero/a: annoying, stronger than *changa* but nicer than *jodón*.

• **los niños hablan cuando las gallinas mean**

🍴 **majarete**: typical pudding-like dessert generally served sprinkled with cinnamon.

🍴 **malanga**: a type of root vegetable.

malcriao: poorly raised, without manners.

malecón: a boardwalk.

mamao: looks like an idiot or imbecile.

mameluco: overalls.

mamey: 1. a type of fruit 2. (syn. *quitado*) something easy.

★ **mami**: 1. an affectionate term for a loved one, 2. a hot babe.

mamito: see *bonitillo*.

💣 **mamizonga**: term for a gorgeous women, a knock-out.

maña: astuteness.

mañana pones: excuse me.

mancha de plátano: a Puerto Rican.

mandar madre: said of something exceptionally difficult.

mandulete: (syn. *manganzón*) a tramp, vagrant, bum, "lazy bones."

manganzón: see *mandulete*.

mangar/mangao: to catch someone doing something wrong.

★🍴 **mangó**: mango fruit.

mangonear: to not do anything, to be a vagrant.

mano: brother, in a slang sense, used among friends.

manos a la obra: get to work.

☺**mapo**: a mop.

☺**mapiar**: to mop.

mapuchado: covered, hidden, disguised.

maquinilla: typewriter.

maquinón: bitchin' wheels.

marayojunda: a term used to express frustration.

marinerito sobre cubierta: cough it up, show me how you will pay for this, how you will be able to accomplish this, phrase used to question one's (financial) ability to finish or maintain something or someone else.

mariquita: a long, thin fried chip, made from plantains or other root vegetables cut lengthwise, similar to a potato chip.

★ **marquesina**: car garage.

★ **más nada** (pr. *má ná*): nothing else. (see Grammar Section).

★ **más ninguno**: nothing else, nothing more.

★ **mata**: any type of plant.

matahambre: a snack, literally "hunger killer."

matapiojos: a persistent or tenacious person.

matarse: 1. to sacrifice oneself doing something. 2. to wipe out.

¿mataste a quien te estaba matando?: question asking if you have eaten.

matojo: in the middle of no where, the boonies.

★ **me cago en nada** (pr. *mé ká wé ná*): damn, shit; expletive used when you forget something or did something incorrectly, also used to express surprise or frustration.

★ **me caso en ná (me caso en nada)**: the polite form of *me cago en nada*.

me comió un caballo: to get badly beaten in a competition.

◆ **me cago en nada**

¿me das el sí?: to ask someone to go steady with you or be your girlfriend.

me dieron calabaza: to get dumped.

me sacan de carrera: (syn. *sacarle de quicio*) to make someone lose his temper or lose control.

💣 **mea'o**: pissed off, really angry.

💣 **mear**: to piss.

media naranja: one's perfect match, in a romantic sense.

melaza: something good.

melena: long hair.

menéalo que se te empelota: phrase used at women that walk with a sway in their hips, would you like fries with that shake?

mengano: see *fulano*.

💣 **mentar la madre**: (syn. *sea la madre*) cuss out one's mother, talk badly of one's mother.

meollo: in the middle of a situation, in the hot seat.

💣 **meter**: to fuck.

meter la cuchara: to jump into or interrupt a conversation.

meter la feca: to tell lies, to fake out, to fake something.

meter las patas: to screw something up, put your foot in your mouth.

★ **meter mano**: 1. literally "put in a hand" referring to "lend a hand" or to start working on something. 2. to sleep with or get it on with someone.

meter un paquete: to lie to someone.

meterle el diente a algo: to roll one's sleeves up and get involved with a difficult task.

meterse en ruta: to go out partying.

meterse por los ojos: to sell something to the point of being pushy.

meterle un mongo: to achieve something by subtle and persuasive means.

metido en el baúl: see *en el baúl*.

mezclar la gimnasia con la magnesia: mixing apples and oranges.

m'hijo, mijo, mijito: terms of endearment between people;

contractions made from "mi hijo/a" and mean "my son" or "my daughter"; are not necessarily used only with one's children.

mi capu: used to allude maliciously to someone without directly naming the person.

mime: small, annoying insect that stings (like a gnat or mosquito).

minguinguingui: a meaningless phrase used by Vicente Martínez, a well-known makeover artist, stylist and Puerto Rican personality.

miqueo: see *guame*.

mira para allá (pronounced mira pa ya): literally "look at that", an exp. of incredulation or surprise.

☺ **mitin**: a meeting, especially a political rally.

mocho/a: amputated.

mocoso: a baby.

★ ◉ **mofongo**: a typical Puerto Rican dish prepared with mashed green (not ripe) plantain; served alone as a side dish or mixed with seafood, chicken, pork.

mogolla: a complicated or difficult situation, "a sticky situation".

💩 **mojón, mojona**: a turd, also used in reference to a person.

💩 **mojonear**: to waste time or screw off.

mollero: buff, built, strong.

☺ **monchis**: the munchies, a desire to eat sweets or snack food.

mondar: to peel fruit.

★ **monga**: a common cold.

montar tribuna: describes someone that gives a long, unprepared, improvised speech about a topic that comes up in conversation.

móntate en un clavo caliente: Buzz off!, Split!, Leave!

morir con las botas puestas: to be very stubborn or headstrong, stick to a position even though it is proven wrong, hang on until the end.

moros en la costa: people can overhear or eavesdrop.

morra: weakness, sickness, tiredness.

★ **morriña**: the fuzziness or cobwebs in the head that one experiences when first waking up.

morrisqueta: funny face.

muá: sound used to signify a kiss.

mucha mecha, poca dinamita: all bark and no bite, a lot of words but no action.

mucho Santacló y poco Thanksgiving: used to describe someone that likes to receive gifts without reciprocating.

★ **muecas**: to make faces, see *cucas monas*.

♦ **mucha mecha, poca dinamita**

muerto de hambre: a loser, a bum, a nobody.

★ **muerto de la risa**: dying from laughter.

muerto el pollo: all wrapped up, finished, done.

mujeriego: see *enamorao*.

mundial: unique, in a bad sense.

mundillo: traditional hand woven lace, mostly from the western portion of Puerto Rico.

¡murió!: exp. to cut off a conversation or used to close abruptly a pending matter.

N

nacariles del oriente: No way!, Forget it!

nacer parao: to have luck in life.

nada más con el testigo: to confirm something that was in question or doubt.

🍽 **ñame**: type of root vegetable.

ñangotao: alt. sp. of *eñangotao*.

ñapa: extra.

ñaqui: a bit of something.

necio: stupid, fool, idiot, brute, see *sángano*.

negro: an endearing term for "honey","dear", or "sweetie"; this term has nothing to do with the race of the person, and in no way has any derogatory connection.

ni fu ni fa: to not care one way or the other.

ni fu ni fi: neither one thing nor the other.

ni modo: to not have another option.

★ **ni pa**: used to mean "no way" or "don't even think about it."

ni pito ni flauta: to have no right to be involved, to mind one's own business.

★☺ **nice**: nice, nifty, cool.

★ **nítido**: cool, good, neat.

no aparecer ni en los centros espiritistas: to disappear without a trace.

no casarse con nadie: 1. exp. to indicate someone with a strong, independent character, 2. to treat everyone equally, not play favorites.

no comer cuento: to not be fearful of anything.

no creer ni en la luz eléctrica: phrase used to refer to extreme skepticism.

no dar pie con bola: to not have the ability to do something, incompetent.

no dar un tajo: to not lend a hand, not help at all.

no decir ni ji: to not talk, not say a word, to not speak out when given the opportunity or when one should protest.

★**no encontrar dónde pararse**: not have a foot to stand on, an indefensible position.

no entiende ni papa: clueless, doesn't understand or follow what is happening.

no es lo mismo ni se escribe igual: phrase to highlight that two things are not equal.

no es lo mucho sino lo continuo: (syn. *no es lo mucho sino lo seguidito*) a pain in the neck, someone that is always bothersome or annoying.

no es lo mucho sino lo seguidito: see *no es lo mucho sino lo continuo*.

★ **no es para tanto**: phrase used to express that someone's reaction was exaggerated or overboard.

no es santo de su devoción: to not be liked by someone, to not be a fan of.

no estoy en mi gallinero: phrase used to avoid giving an opinion, to stay out of the middle of squabbles or arguments when one is asked to take sides.

no extrañar gallera: to fit in or be in one's element anywhere.

no habla por no ofender: exp. to describe someone excessively timid or discreet.

no le duele nada: to be very good-looking.

no lo quiero ver ni en pintura: to be so fed up with or disgusted by someone that one does not want to ever see them again.

★ **no me fuñas**: don't bother me, don't bug me.

no me quiero para nada: to not care what happens to oneself, to the point of willing to die.

no olerle a alguien ni las azucenas: to be in bad humor, to not be animated.

no para la pata: an eternal traveler, someone that is never at home, someone always on the road.

★ **no pare más**: that's it, there's nothing else.

★ **no pegar ni una**: to not get anything right, to be way off.

no pegarse ni bailando: to have bad luck in relation to games of chance.

no perderle ni pie ni pisá: to stick to someone like a shadow, like white on rice.

no quedarse sin bueyes para arar: to not put all the eggs in one basket.

no quitarle el guante de la cara: to accost or harass.

no rendir promedio: to not work out properly.

no saber un divino: to know nothing.

no se va a quedar dado: a person is going to look for revenge, the person will not stay quiet, will not accept what has happened without reacting.

no ser cáscara de coco: not be something easy to resolve.

no te hagas el mosquito muerto: pretending to be a nice person in order to trick someone.

• **no quitarle el guante de la cara**

no te pegues, que no es bolero: phrase used to let someone know that they are too close, that they are invading your personal space.

no te salva ni el médico chino: someone has reached the end of the line, there's no way out, it's all over.

no te vistas que no vas: you will not achieve your goal, emphasizes that someone has not been included, selected or has not won.

no tiene pasta para eso: to not be right or cut out for something.

no tiene pelos en la lengua: (syn. *no tiene pepitas en la lengua*) to get straight to the point, to not mince words, to be very frank, straightforward or direct.

no tiene pepitas en la lengua: see *no tiene pelos en la lengua*.

no tiene vela en este entierro: mind one's own business.

no tienen en qué caerse muerto: broke, bankrupt, insolvent..

★ **Nuyorican**: the term used for New Yorkers of Puerto Rican descent; many of these people were born in New York and have never lived in Puerto Rico but still maintain close familial ties to the island.

O

o te peinas o te haces rolos: used to push someone to make a decision.

¡oficial!: without a shadow of a doubt, sure.

 oler a puta: literally "to smell like a whore", used for someone that uses too much or a really strong perfume.

olla de grillos: a hotbed of tension.

olvídese de los peces de color: don't worry about it, don't lose any sleep over it.

★ **otros veinte pesos**: "that's a whole different story."

P

p' atrás: phrase to mean it's a lie or untrue.

pa' encima, Lola: bring it on!, let's fight!, let's go!

pachó: embarassed, shamed.

pachosa: timid.

pai: pa, dad, pops.

pajitas que le caen a la leche: minor problems, trivialities, "it's nothing".

pajuato: a fool.

palitos: sticks used for music in typical Puerto Rican music.

★ **palo**: 1. an alcoholic drink. 2. a tree.

palo limpio: to kick someone's ass, to beat someone up.

pan comido: something easy.

🍽 **pana**: 1. breadfruit, 2. friend, buddy, pal.

🍽 **panapén**: breadfruit.

pantaletas: panties.

pantalones: guts, balls.

papá: man, dude.

papear: to eat.

papel: 100 dollar bill.

★ **papi**: 1. used as an affectionate term for a loved one, 2. daddy, papa.

papi chulo: a cute, handsome, attractive man.

papujo: swollen from being hit, from an allergy or disease.

paquetero: a liar.

para allí para abajo: (syn. *por allí para abajo*) straight ahead for a while, keep going.

para salir del paso: a quick fix, to do something to just to finish it even if it was not done well or properly.

para viejo, yo: means that the speaker will only date younger people, if there's anyone old around, it is going to be me.

💣 **parabicho**: a dick-tease.

pararle el caballo/caballito: to contain, control or keep under moderation.

pararlo en seco: to stop someone dead in their tracks, to stop someone cold, to put an abrupt end to any ideas.

★🍽 **parcha**: passion fruit.

parece que no rompe un plato pero rompe la vajilla: someone is pretending to be nice to get away with something.

parece un pastel mal envuelto: fat, overweight.

☛**parejero**: see *comemierda*.

parió la mula: so what!, big deal!

★☺ **parisear**: to party, to go out.

★☺ **parking**: a parking space, a parking garage, any type of place to park.

★☺ **parquear**: to park.

parranda: a night out on the town.

pasar con ficha: to come out well from a difficult situation.

pasar el macho: 1. to waste time, 2. to mess around with someone sexually.

pasar el rolo: in an assembly approve or reject something by an overwhelming majority.

pasar el taco: to come out of a difficult or disagreeable situation.

pasar raspa cum laude: to pass a class or exam by the minimum required.

pasarle la mano a alguien: to flatter someone to calm them down or to butter them up.

pasarse de la raya: to cross the line, to the point of being disrespectful.

pasarse de listo: to believe you are smarter or more clever than other people, without really being so.

★ **pasiar**: to go out and wander around.

pasmarse: to be frozen from surprise, shocked.

pasto: dope, marijuana.

patidifusa: surprised.

patiflaco: thin legs, stick legs.

patinarle el coco: to be nutty, crazy.

☛ **pato**: queer, homosexual.

pava: 1. a type of hat, 2. the political party "*Partido Popular*".

pavera: to laugh hysterically, especially among teenagers.

pedir cacao: to give up, to surrender.

pegacuernos, pegar cuernos: to cheat on (one's romantic partner).

🍴 **pegado**: 1. the burned part of the rice in the bottom of a pot, considered a delicacy, 2. "in", cool, *Ex. musicians.*

pegar: to guess correctly.

★ **pegar a (hacer algo)**: to begin something.

pegar con alguien: to blame someone.

pegar el diente: to eat voraciously.

pegar un vellón: to bother or make fun of someone.

pegarse la frisa: to oversleep.

pela: a whoopin', a beating or to beat up on.

pelambrera: to be broke, penniless.

pelea de tigre y burro: a lopsided fight.

♠ **pellejo**: 1. whore. 2. pieces of skin (ex. hangnail) that can be pulled off.

pellizco de ñoco: something that isn't easy.

pelo a pelo: phrase that means to be an even match, an even deal or fair trade.

pelo chorreado: extremely straight hair.

pelota, pelotero: literally "ball", in contrast to many other Latin American countries where this means soccer, in Puerto Rico this is a reference to baseball.

★ **pelú**: 1. see *greñú.* 2. to be really cold.

pendango/a: (syn. *pendejo*) idiot, sucker.

★♠ **pendejo/a**: see *pendango.*

penepé: refers to the political party PNP, *Partido Nuevo Progresista*, one of the main political parties in Puerto Rico.

pensar en pajaritos preñaos: to be distracted, literally "to think about pregnant birds".

♠ **peo**: a fart.

pepa: force or vigor.

Pepino: the town of San

Sebastian.

peposo: "yummy" in reference to a person or something else.

percha: a closet hanger.

perder la chaveta: to lose one's temper or patience, to blow up, to explode.

perencejo: see *fulano*.

perico: sl. for cocaine.

★ **perreo**: a "doggy style" dance that earned its name for the way two people dance together.

pesado: tiring.

★ **peseta**: a 25-cent coin, a quarter.

peseta voladora: so what, big deal.

peso: refers to a US dollar, the official currency. *Peso* is used interchangeably with *dólar*.

🍽 **petit pois**: peas.

pícalo, gallo!: exp. Keep it up!, Keep going!, Way to go!

picar fuera del hoyo: to be wrong.

pichón: 1. a guy's wiener, 2. a bird.

picúa: flirtatious.

pileta: wash tub.

🍽 **pilones**: lollipops

• **perder la chaveta**

pimienta en el salero: a partier, the life of the party.

piña: a knock or rap on the head.

★ ‖●‖ **pincho**: a skewer of beef, shrimp, chicken or other meat.

pintar: to leave quickly, rapidly or right away.

★ ‖●‖ **pionono**: mature plaintain stuffed with ground beef, formed into a hockey-puck shape, and fried.

pipa, pipón: tummy.

pipi: 1. a penis. 2. to pee. The term *pipi* is socially acceptable to use with kids.

★ ‖●‖ **pique**: hot sauce, often homemade.

piquita: easy money, a cushy job.

‖●‖ **piragua**: a snow cone.

piropo: a phrase to complement a woman about her looks, sometimes in an aggressive or sexual manner; a *piropo* can range from a complement about the color of a woman's eyes to a very explicit sexual comment about a body part; depending on the sincerity and intent of the comment it can be received

several ways: graciously, without comment or even with a slap in the face.

‖●‖ **pirulí**: a type of candy.

pisar la comida con algo: to wash down food with an alcoholic beverage.

pisarle el rabo a alguien: to figuratively sit down somewhere immediately after someone else has left.

pisicorre: a small bus used especially in the mountains of Puerto Rico to go between towns.

pisotear: to squash, step on, talk poorly of a person.

pistolita sin inscribir: a smart aleck, a wise guy.

pitirre: a type of bird.

‖●‖ **pitorro**: a type of liquor, moonshine.

‖●‖ **plantilla**: 1. a tortilla, 2. bottom of shoe.

plantón: the act of standing someone up.

●‖ **plasta**: shit, vagrant, worthless.

plástico: proud.

platanutre: a fried chip made from plaintain, similar to potato chip or *mariquita*.

plenero: a type of music.

pollina: the bangs of the hair.

polvorones: a type of almond shortbread.

pompis: rear end, butt, butt cheeks.

☺ **ponchar**: to stamp something, to punch a time card.

poner a alguien como chupa de china: to insult someone.

poner a uno a beber: to bribe or buy off someone.

poner los cuernos: to cheat on (one's partner), literally "to put the horns on".

poner un huevo: to make a mistake.

poner un huevo cuadrado: to make a big mistake, literally to lay a square egg.

ponerlo a gozar: to give someone enjoyment, pleasure.

ponerse a'lante: to be the rage, the latest fashion, the most desirable.

ponerse bellaco: to be sexually excited.

ponerse bondo: to apply too much makeup, to have cosmetic surgery.

ponerse como pimpo: to be stuffed with food or drink.

ponerse en algo: to act in accordance with others, or with the current fashion or trend.

ponerse las botas: to do something in excess.

ponerse puerquito: to pay, to make very generous invitations.

ponerse en cuatro: assume the doggy style position

♦ **poner un huevo cuadrado**

sexually, similar to *hacer posición cuatro*.

ponle pichón: forget it, don't pay attention to it.

ponte listo: think about what you are going to do.

ponte pá tu número (ponte para tu número): get in touch with reality, reality check, don't forget who you are.

ponte pálido: ante up, pay up, pick up the check, invite everyone else.

por allí para abajo: see *para allí para abajo*.

por amor al arte: sarcastic form of saying that one does not work for free.

por debajo de la mesa: to do something under the table, in a hidden manner, illegally.

por donde más le duele: literally "where it hurts most", take action where the person will feel it most.

por la maceta: outstanding or excellent.

por relajar: jokingly.

por si aca (por si acaso): short way of saying *por si acaso* or just in case.

por si las moscas: just in case.

por un tubo y siete llaves: refers to a large quantity.

porqueria: something that has little or no value.

pote 'e leche: lilly white.

potoroca: food that the government distributed.

prángana: broke (money), penniless.

★ **preñá (preñada)**: pregnant (for a woman), in Spanish this word is normally used for animals instead of people.

prender de un maniguetazo: to be angry.

prensá: pretty, attractive.

🍽 **preparadito**: this is a round Puerto Rican pastry made from puff pastry with ham and cheese inside; normally eaten as a snack or for breakfast.

presentao: see *averiguao* or *entrometido*.

primero llueve p' arriba: literally "first it will rain upwards", when pigs fly, never.

★☺ **printear**: to print from a computer.

procurar por alguien: to ask for someone.

prometer villas y castillas: to sweet-talk someone, to promise someone the world and then not deliver.

puertorro: a Puerto Rican.

pujar un coco: to put out a real strong effort to achieving something, without achieving it.

★●✲ **puñeta**: literally "jerk off", but also used as all around expletive (ex. whenever you hurt yourself).

puño: a punch.

púyala, púyala!: phrase used to motivate people to move on or move forward.

Q

★ **qué chavienda!**: What a pain!, What a bother!, How ridiculous!

★ **qué chévere!**: Wonderful!, How nice!, How cool!

qué come libro: How studious!

¿qué es lo tuyo?: "What's your thing?", what are you about?, what are you proposing?

¡qué fallo, líder!: an expresion used to make fun of someone that has made a very visible or obvious mistake.

¡qué ganso!: what a slimeball!, what a shifty person!

¡qué guiso!: something that earns good money without a lot of effort.

¡qué huevo!: screwup.

¡qué lengua!: what a gossip!

¡qué macho!: exp. used to communicate admiration for someone's courage or bravery.

¿Que máh? (que más): What else?

que mosquero!: how boring!, to be out of the loop, to not be in the know.

que no pase de aquí: keep this secret.

que pantalones!: what right do you have!, the nerve!

¡que peste a mangle!: it stinks here, it reaks, it smells bad.

que pisa y no arranca: to start something without finishing it or following through.

¿qué pito toca?: what does this do?, what part does this have?

¿qué tú comes que adivinas?: phrase used when someone completes another's sentence or when someone says what another person is about to say.

quedar más que uno: to have only one left; the correct spanish phrase is *quedar solamente uno*.

quedar sembrao: literally "to be seeded", means to accommodate oneself or to stay in the same place.

quedar seteao: to be ready (for the next step) or set up.

quedarse como palo: to fall asleep.

quedarse como yuca: to fall asleep.

quedarse guindando: stood up.

quedarse jamona: to be an old maid, a single women beyond marrying age.

quedársele en una muela: to still be hungry after eating.

★ ❙◉❙ **quesito**: a breakfast pastry made from a thin dough, filled with cream cheese, with sugar crystals sprinkled on top.

¿quién le pone el cascabel al gato?: phrase used after giving someone advice that is ignored and the situation evolves exactly as predicted.

¿quién te hace rico? El que te mantiene el pico: phrase that criticizes a freeloader, especially someone that has the means to support himself, but prefers to receive from others to save his own (money, food, etc.)

quijá: chin.

★ **quitado**: something easy or simple to do, a given. *Ex. Este trabajo es un quitado, te lo entrego ahora mismo.*

quítate tú para ponerme yo: get out of the way, I'm taking over.

R

rabo del ojo: the corner of the eye (glancing at someone from the corner of the eye, as if not to look).

rajar la papeleta: in an election, vote for candidates all from the same party.

rajarse: to not finish something.

★☺ **ranqueao (ranqueado)**- literally "ranked", of an upper level or first place.

★☺ **rapero/a**: rapper.

rapiar: to conquer (a woman).

raquítico: skinny.

raspacoco: a short haircut (as in military recruits).

raspando: scratching along, just barely.

💣 **rasparse la paja**: to jerk off.

realengo: from the street, homeless, a stray.

rechonchón: a senior citizen party animal.

recoge tus motetes y vete: get out, leave immediately, you're fired!

recogerse a buen vivir: after a period of great excitement, remain at home or lead a calm life, grow up and act like an adult.

★ **regañar**: 1. to spoil, 2. to scold.

reguerete: (syn. *reguero*) a mess, a disaster, thrown around.

reguero: see *reguerete*.

reírse con las muelas de atrás: sarcastically, hypocritically.

★ **relajo/ relajar/ relajando**: joke, to joke, joking.

renacuajo: the runt of a litter.

repartir el bacalao: divide the workload.

residencial: public housing.

retahíla: a long line.

reventado: wiped out, exhausted.

★🍽 **revoltillo**: scrambled eggs.

★ **revolú**: (syn. *vacilón*) a mess, a mix-up, pandemonium.

robarse el show: steal the show.

rollo: a mess.

rompecunas: cradle robber; a person dating someone much younger.

romper hielo: literally "to break the ice."

romper la noche: to stay up all night.

🍽 **ron caña**: a type of alcoholic drink made from sugarcane, similar to rum, moonshine.

ronquera de mozo: a hoarse voice, or a boy's changing voice in puberty.

☺ **rostizar**: to roast.

S

★ **sabrá Dios**: God knows!, who knows, phrase used to express doubt.

sacar el buey de la barranca: to execute a difficult task.

sacar el chinchorro: fish with a net and the process of pulling in the fish.

sacar el cuerpo: to avoid someone.

sacar en cara: to rub something in someone's face.

sacar los pies del plato: to solve a problem, to resolve something, to find a solution.

sacar pecho: to challenge someone, to strut around, to stand up to someone.

sacarle de quicio: see *me sacan de carrera*.

sacarle el jugo: (syn. *sacarle el mondogo*) to exploit or take advantage of something.

sacarle el mondogo: see *sacarle el jugo*.

sacarle punta a las cosas: to nit-pick, to fight everything, to be an obstacle to change, to resist everything.

sacarle un hijo macho: to obtain a huge favor from someone.

sacarse de la manga: to make up or invent, at that moment, "by the seat of your pants", "pull out of thin air".

sacarse el gordo: to win the lottery.

sácate ese juey que tienes en el bolsillo: stop being a cheapskate.

¡sacude, zapato viejo!: get lost!, go away!, get outta here!

sal si puede: (syn. *un corre y corre*) all hell breaking loose, a rush or stampede of people.

salado: unlucky, jinxed.

💣 **salir cagao a alguien (salir cagado a alguien)**: to look exactly like one's father or mother.

salir de oro: to come out ahead or benefited in a matter.

salir del hoyo: escape from a difficult matter or a poor financial situation.

salirle a uno con una parantolá: to respond rudely or impolitely to someone.

🍽 **salmorejo**: a typical Puerto Rican dish generally made from crab, similar to a thick soup with a tomato base, often spicy.

salpafuera: a hostile argument or fight.

sambumbia: bad tasting food.

★ **San Juan**: specifically Old San Juan.

sanana: (syn. *sángano, zángano*) a mild form of *sángano*.

🍽 **sancocho**: a Puerto Rican stew made from root vegetables that may include a type of meat.

sandwich: rear end, heinie.

★ **sángano**: an idiot or fool.

sangrigordo: a bother, a pest, a nuisance.

santo: literally "saint" but is normally used in reference to wood carvings which are hand painted and are used for decoration more so than for religious purposes.

★ **Santo Domingo**: although this is the capital city of the Dominican Republic, this name is used in reference to any part of the country and not only the city.

santo y bueno: acceptable, no problem.

Santo, ¿dónde te pongo?: anything you want, whatever you say goes.

Santo, ¿quieres misa?: of course, you bet, naturally.

sato: 1. a mutt, 2. a slick or slippery person.

se acabó el evento: The End, everything is over so it is time to leave.

se acabó el pan de piquito: means that something good has come to an end.

se acabó lo que se daba: the party's over, lights out.

se aguó la fiesta: the party died out, or got spoiled.

★ **se botó**: to go all out, overboard, beyond the expected or necessary.

se cree la reina del Timbeque: a woman that thinks she is the center of attention, that she is the most important person in the room.

se cree que tiene el gato por el rabo: to believe one has everything under control, to have the horse by the reigns.

sé de la pata de que cojea: to not be fooled by someone.

se deja comer: in reference to food, something that is good but not fantastic.

se están casando las brujas: exp. that refers to when it rains and the sun is out at the same time.

se formó un arroz con pollo: a situation blew up, things got ugly.

★ **se fue ajuste**: to go wrong, to go downhill, to go bankrupt.

se la comió: to do well, to come out ahead.

★ **se las sabe todas**: to know the situation extremely well, to understand all the angles.

se le esbarató el simiñoco: (syn. *se le esbarató la coclaina*) something was injured.

♦ **se cree que tiene el gato por el rabo**

se le esbarató la coclaina: see *se le esbarató el simiñoco.*

se le para la lengua: after one drink, the person wants to continue partying.

se le pasea el alma por el cuerpo: said about someone extremely relaxed, that doesn't react to anything.

se le pegó la sábana: to oversleep.

se le subieron los humos a la cabeza: to have success go to one's head, to begin to think one is more important than others, to expect special treatment.

se le trancó el bolo: to get stuck, to hit a snag.

se le va a caer el kiosko: something (a business, an agreement, etc.) is going to fall apart from lack of support or focus.

se le van a poner los ojos como vaca que va pa' risco: to receive a big surprise, to be shocked.

se le viró la tortilla: to have the tables turned, to have things turned upside-down.

se lo muerde: a cheapskate or tightwad.

se metió en el lío de los pastores: to get mixed up in problems, to have a mess to unravel.

se puso como sapo de letrina: to eat until one is stuffed.

se vistió como la puerca de Juan Bobo: to get all spiffied up, to put on Sunday's best, to get really dressed up.

se volvió un ocho: (syn. *se volvió una crayola*) to be paralyzed by confusion, to be overwhelmed.

se volvió una crayola: see *se volvió un ocho.*

💣 **sea la madre**: see *mentar la madre.*

seguir de rolimpín: to continue the party.

seguir de rolo: to keep on going, without stopping.

¿seguro? Seguro está Dios en los cielos: ironic phrase used to express doubt or skepticism when someone assures that an event will happen.

★ **sendo**: a lot of something.

Ex. Ahora mismo hay <u>sendo</u> tapón en la Martinez Nadal. Parece que dos carros chocaron.

sentar cabeza: to grow up or to act mature.

sentársele encima a algo: to postpone something that it is not beneficial to resolve at the moment.

ser broco: refers to a person missing a hand or arm.

ser canalla: to be cruel.

ser cano: blonde.

ser castao: valiant.

ser el jamón del sandwich: see *estar como el jamón de sandwich.*

ser la changa: to be a bad or clever person that looks to benefit from a negative situation, even at the expense of others.

ser ñoco: refers to a person missing an arm.

💣 **ser patriota**: a woman with large breasts.

ser picoreto: a talkative child.

ser plástico: proud, artificial.

ser por alguien: to protect, take care of or take charge of someone.

ser un afrentao: 1. stingy, everything for oneself, 2. a voracious appetite for food, or other things.

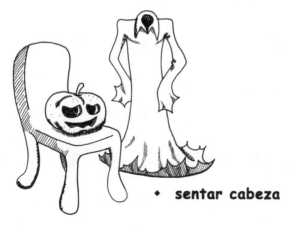

♦ **sentar cabeza**

ser un canto de: a piece of something.

ser un fiebrú: someone that is extremely enthusiastic about something new, but soon after loses interest and abandons it.

ser un güelío: fool, idiot.

ser un lengüetero: a gossip.

ser un mantequilla: a physically weak person.

ser un melao: a sweet or caring person.

ser un metío: a nosy person, someone that sticks their nose where it does not belong.

ser un muerto: merchandise that does not sell.

ser un paracaidista: to crash a party.

♦ **ser un fiebrú**

💣 ☺ **ser un pila de mierda**: literally "a pile of shit", used in reference to someone that is still a child or child-like.

ser un quincallero: a womanizer.

ser un tronco de: a tremendous or extraordinary thing.

ser una batata: to be someone with a cushy or easy job that pays well, often in the government.

ser una dama: a courteous and gentlemanly man.

ser una guerrillera: an easy women.

ser una longaniza: a drawn-out or long-winded speech or written piece.

🍽 **serenata**: a salad of avocado, onion, olive oil and tomato often served with codfish.

serrucho: everyone chips in to buy something.

★ **si Dios quiere**: God willing.

si fuese mudo, estallaría: literally "if he were mute, he would explode", means that a person really wants to jump into a conversation.

¡sí hombe!: yeah dude.

si madura como pinta: the hope that something is resolved as one wishes.

si no es Juan es Pedro: if it's not one thing it is another.

sicote: foot odor.

sigue durmiendo de ese lado: literally "keep sleeping on that side", means that if a person continues to maintain their current opinion or position, he or she will soon be proven wrong.

sigue tú con tu montuno, que yo te veo allá: you continue on your way and I'll continue on mine.

síguelo que está la verde: to (figuratively) have a green light to continue whatever one is doing.

similñoco: a handle for something or contraption.

sin encomendarse a nadie: impulsively.

sin que me quede nada por dentro: literally "without

anything staying within me", to say something with sincerity.

★ **sinverguenza**: a shameless or brazen person. *Ex. Ese sinvergüenza trató de cobrarme 20 pesos cuando realmente vale solamente 15!*

sinsabores: bitter tasting, suffering.

siquitraque: firecracker.

sobaco: armpit.

sobar: to knead or caress (especially in reference to bread, *pan sobao*).

sobrado: a freeloader, a fifth wheel.

sobrajas: leftovers.

★ ⦿ **sofrito**: a type of spice or condiment used in typical Puerto Rican cooking especially with rice.

sombrilla: umbrella.

somos muchos los hijos del muerto: everyone is in the same boat.

son de armas tomadas: someone with a one-track mind, even to the point of being violent, crazy or extreme.

son de la loza: name used by country people for city people.

soñar con pajaritos preñaos: pretend the impossible.

sonero/a: a person that invents lyrics as he/she sings.

sonsacar: to convince someone to do something that he would not normally do.

sonsonete: same thing.

⦿ **soplapote**: an assistant, gofer or aid (derogatory), fool, idiot.

sorbeto: a drinking straw.

⦿ **sorullo**: cornmeal which is shaped into short, fat sticks and fried; often an appetizer.

sosa: 1. flavorless, 2. worn out, run down, tired.

subió como la espuma: a star performer, a fast mover, someone that has moved up the corporate ladder rapidly.

subir y bajar santos: to blaspheme, to cuss.

sudar la gota gorda: to work.

sudar la patria: to work excessively.

suelto como un gabete: literally "as loose as a shoe string"; means to be out of control, wild, crazy or partying incessantly.

★ **sultano**: see *fulano*.

suruma: hard-headed.

☺ **swing**: movement in the hips related to dancing.

T

taco: a nice or sweet person.

talar: to put someone in his place, to cut someone down to size.

tantas curvas y yo sin freno: a *piropo,* a comment made to beautiful women when seen in public, literally "so many curves and me without brakes."

◆ **tantas curvas y yo sin freno**

tapaíto: comes from *tapado*, to cover up; used when someone is trying to hide something or trying to keep something low key.

★ **tapón**: traffic jam.

te cojo bajando: to get revenge, to "catch up with someone", payback.

te digo ahorita: a phrase used to postpone eternally a subject or topic.

te lleva para lo hondo: someone is taking advantage of you, pulling the wool over your eyes.

te lo vendo como me lo vendieron: I'll tell you exactly as it was told to me.

¿te pica el coco?: are you crazy?, are you nuts?

te tiene y no te suelta: someone has complete control over you, knows which buttons to push to control you.

te traje con el pensamiento: literally "I brought you with the thought", means speak of the devil, used when someone appears unexpectedly and was the topic of conversation.

te vas a buscar un pinche: to be looking for trouble.

★☺ **te veo**: literally "see you", means see you later.

tecato: 1. a drug addict, 2. drugged.

temblar como un novato: to shake like a leaf.

🍽 **tembleque**: a white gelatin-like dessert, often with cinnamon sprinkled on top.

tener a alguien sentado en el baúl: a husband who is dominated by his wife.

tener babilla: to have courage.

tener buen diente: to have a strong appetite.

tener chichos: to have rolls of fat on the body.

tener el banco virao: to have a lot of money.

tener el pelo pasú: to have curly hair.

tener gusto de rico y bolsillo de pobre: to have expensive tastes without the means to maintain them.

💣 **tener hormigas en el culo**: (syn. *tener hormigas en el* *fondillo*) "ants in your pants", anxious, hyperactive, nervous.

tener hormigas en el fondillo: the mild form of *tener hormigas en el culo*.

tener la música por dentro: a quiet, reserved person, that livens up whenever there's a party.

tener la piel finita: to be very susceptible thin-skinned.

tener más leche que un palo de pana: to be very lucky or affortunate.

tener mucho queso: to have a wide forehead.

tener rasquiña de mono: to have the habit of scratching oneself frequently, like a monkey.

tener un coco con alguien: to be in love with someone.

tener un lambío de vaca: to comb one's hair very flat.

tener un ñame: to have a huge foot, the size of a *ñame* vegetable.

tener un vellón pegado: annoyed, pissed.

tener una agenda escondida: to have a hidden agenda.

tener una cara como que le deben y no le pagan: someone has a very serious or angry exp. on his face.

tener una pala: to have influence.

tener una papa caliente en las manos: to have a hot potato in one's hands, to have a difficult problem.

tenerle un lado seco a alguien: fed up with always bailing someone out.

★ **tenis**: 1. tennis shoes, 2. the sport tennis.

★ 👄 **tetas**: tits.

time ball: time out, when playing a game.

tipo/a: a guy or gal, dude, chick, etc.

🍴 **tira y jala**: a stretchy caramel bar made with cream of coconut.

tirar bomba: to stand someone up.

tirar la toalla: to help.

tirar por la culata: to turn out poorly.

tirarle una cascarita a ver si resbala: give him enough rope and he'll hang himself.

tirarse al desperdicio: to prostitute oneself.

tirarse de pecho: Go ahead!, Jump in head first!, Go for it!

tirarse la maroma: see *dispararse la maroma*.

tirijala: a mess.

títere: a punk or juvenile delinquent.

★ **titi**: auntie. *Ex. La casa de Titi Wanda en Lares es enorme.*

titingó: a fight, squabble, discussion.

toda la vida y un mes más: literally "life-long and one more month", forever.

todavía: not yet, different from gramatically correct Spanish in which it means "still".

tomar la batuta: to take responsibility or control of.

tomar el pelo: to tease someone, to take advantage off.

torombolo: a mentally slow person, an idiot, a nitwit.

tostao (tostado) : crazy, nutty.

★ ▮●▮ **tostón**: 1. a mess or screw up, 2. flattened fried plaintain, served as a side dish for local cuisine, 3. a term used with girls to refer to their private parts.

▮●▮ **tostonera**: cooking device used to make tostones.

trabajar como blanco: to not do anything, in reference to working like a white man (as opposed to a slave, who works a lot).

trabajar con los pies: not be very effective or productive, everything that one produces is poor quality.

♦ **trabajar con los pies**

trancado: used in reference to the game dominoes when both sides of the game have the same number and there are no legal plays left; a player generally freezes the game on purpose this way.

traquetero, traquetear, traqueteo: something not completely legal, a shady deal.

trastornada: crazy, nutty.

tremenda mami: "hot mama", an attractive women.

★ **tremendo**: unbelievable, amazing.

trepadora: a woman that is interested in someone only for his money.

trigueña: someone dark-skinned (tan or olive color).

★ **trililí**: something cheap, not well made.

trilla: out for spin, a ride.

trinco: physically not flexible (ex. body builders).

★☺ **tripear**: 1. from the English "to trip", to hallucinate,

to be confused, 2. to tease or make fun of, to joke about.

trompetilla: to make fun of or mock someone, especially by sticking out your tongue and making noises.

tronado: crazy, insane.

☺ **troses**: trucks.

trulla: music carolers, especially for Christmas.

★☺ **tú sabes**: from the English "you know", used in the same context.

tufo: a stink or smell, bad breath from alcohol.

tumbar(se): 1. to knock over, fall over, 2. to turn off or shut off, 3. to steal or rob.

turca: stumbling drunk.

turuleco: senile or forgetful from old age.

tusa: a moron, riff-raff, a loser.

★ **tutiplén**: a lot of or too much of something, giving away something without care.

U

¡Uepria!: exp. used in surprise.

uípiti: expresses surprise or happiness.

último grito de la moda: the newest craze or rage, the most fashionable.

un bombo al pitcher: something really easy to do, a "freebee."

un canto, cantito: a bit, a piece of.

★ **un día de estos**: one of these days.

un dime y te diré: a gossip session.

★ **un montón**: a lot, a whole bunch.

★ **un palo**: a resounding success. *Ex. El lanzamiento de nuestro nuevo producto fue un palo ya que todos lo compraron de inmediato.*

un pasito pa'lante y dos pa'trás: one step forward and two steps back, not making progress.

un pollo, pollo: cute, handsome.

una mano a'lante y la otra atrás: flat broke.

una trillita: a short ride.

◆ **un bombo al pitcher**

uña y carne: intimate friends, best friends.

unjú: it's like oo hoo, when you catch someone doing something they shouldn't be doing.

untarle a uno la mano: to bribe someone.

Uuuuy no, caca: No not that, it's nasty.

V

va en coche y va en coche: to be lucky with what one received or obtained.

va viento en popa: everything is going well.

★ **vacilar**: to tease or make fun of.

★ **vacilón**: a party, a great time; also see *revolú*.

vaivén: a snafu, problem or hassle.

vaquero: valiant.

velar: to spie on.

★ **vellón**: term used for a nickel or dime (in Ponce).

✆ **venir**: to come, to reach orgasm.

ventiúnica: the only.

ver la luna: to menstruate.

vestida de novia: literally "a bride's dress", refers to a bottle of beer so cold that there is ice on the outside of the bottle.

vieja viruta: (syn. *viejo verde*) an older person that thinks himself young; used in reference to a person dating someone much younger.

viejo chocho: a senile or forgetful old man.

viejo/a verde: see *vieja viruta*.

viroldo: a strange or weird person.

vivir del cuento: embellish stories to con someone, avoid working by lying to people to earn their sympathy.

vivir del mantengo: to live off of government handouts.

vivito y coleando: alive and kicking.

volado: crazy, daffy, strange, weird.

volar bajito: to be about to cross the line, in insulting someone.

voy a hacer que hago: an indirect way of saying "let me continue with what I was doing."

W

wakala: yuck.

Weeepaaa!: like "Woohoo", an exp. of excitement, joy, pleasure.

★☺ **wiken**: literally weekend; this is an english word which has been converted to a spanish spelling.

Y

y: when saying the letter Y it is sometimes pronounced as Jé.

★ **¡y cuidao!**: used to indicate that something may be underestimated. *Ex. Yo creo que llegué a las tres de la mañana ayer, ¡y cuidao!*

y malo: joking phrase in response to someone giving you what you requested, "It's a good thing you did."

¡y para qué fue eso!: and then what happened is...

y tu abuela, adonde está?: phrase used to question someone's claim that they are white or Caucasian, especially when the person shows characteristics of other races.

ya tú sabes: you know how it is, same old story. *Ex. ¿Por qué se divorciaron si todo estaba bien hace 6 meses? Ya tú sabes, él tenía una chilla por allí.*

ya yo ya: already done, finished.

yal: woman, chick.

 yautía: a root vegetable served mashed and in other Puerto Rican cuisine.

yerna: daughter-in-law.

yuntas: cuff-links.

Z

★ **zafacón**: 1. trash can, 2. a whole lot of something.

zafar: to escape, to slip out.

★ **zángano**: alt. sp. of *sángano*.

zapatearse: to pass the buck, avoid the blame.

zoruma: see *sángano*.

♦ **zángano**

Bibliografía/ Bibliography

Deliz Hernández, Joseph: **How To Speak Puerto Rican**, VB Publishing, 1998.

Díaz Rivera, María Elisa: **Refranes más usados en Puerto Rico**, 2nd Edition, Editorial de la Universidad de Puerto Rico, 2002.

García Santos, Nelson: **Lo que dice la gente**, 1997.

Núñez de Ortega, Rosario and Delgado de Laborde, Isabel: **Los que dicen ¡ay bendito!**, 3rd Edition, Editorial Plaza Mayor, 2001.